GOLDENEYE'S FL

THE CO
TOP 10

GOLDENEYE

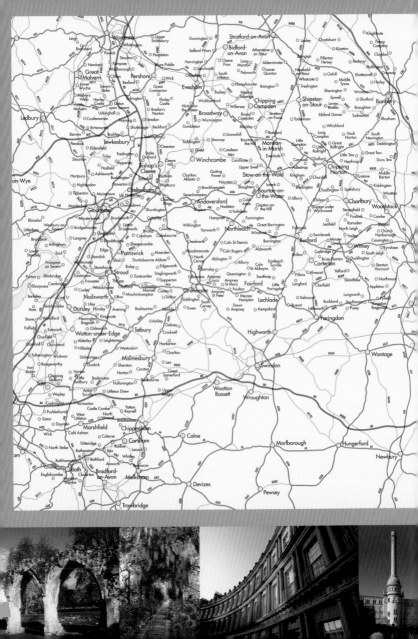

This little book is a condensed version of Goldeneye's Cotswold Guidebook. Goldeneye have been publishing Cotswold Travel Guides, in various formats for 30-years, and this is the first time a Top 10 has been indentified by us. The Top 10 chosen, in each category, has not been done lightly and, it may well be, that these are not to everyone's taste. In an Age when time is at a premium, and when the modern travelller seeks only the best, and is given to short breaks, it seems an apposite moment to publish this book. Those chosen are included on merit, and merit alone. We gain no advertising revenue from them for appearing in this book. We do, however, welcome your feedback.

What and where is the region known as the Cotswolds? To those who know it, this may seem like a silly question. However, it is a place that manifests itself in many different ways to different people. Even down to the area they would define as the Cotswolds on a map. To some fashionistas, and magazine editors, the Cotswolds runs comparison to the New York Hamptons and Tuscany. Whilst to others the name is synonymous with wool and hunting, stone walls and majestic churches. From my point of view and for the purposes of this book, the area stretches from Chipping Campden in the north to Bath in the south, and from Gloucester to Woodstock, west to east. Given the restriction on space, only the town of Bath, and Bath Abbey are described – for to give Bath its full measure, it deserves a book in itself.

The Cotswolds derives its name from two Saxon words: 'Cote' - sheep fold, and 'Wold' - bare hill. This references the importance of sheep in the development of the area. And, it is to the Cotswold Lion sheep that one must look to for the origin of wealth and endeavour that brought prosperity to this region.

The Cotswolds region is perched on the central section of a ridge of oolitic limestone. The geological structure has thus had a profound and lasting affect on the landscape, and 'look' of the area. The oolitic limestone that forms these hills has the appearance of 1,000s of tiny balls, like fish roe and is between 200 and 175 million years old.

This ridge has been tilted on its side and is run off with streams and river valleys that lead off in a south-easterly direction to feed the Thames basin. On the western edge the scarp is steep in places with outcrops of rounded hills, notably Cam Long Down and Bredon Hill and makes for fine walking country and pleasing views across to the Malvern Hills and Wales

Neolithic Man found refuge on these hills from the swamps of the Severn and Thames flood plains. The Celtic Dobunni tribe established hill forts where they farmed, bartered their crafts and founded coinage before the Romans arrived. They were not a warlike tribe like their neighbours the Silurians (Welsh) and eased into a compatible relationship with the conquering Romans to build Corinium Dobunnorum (Cirencester) into the second largest Roman settlement in Britain with a populace of 12,000 inhabitants.

The Saxon farmer laid the foundations of prosperity for the medieval wool merchants, and it was these merchants who built the great 'Wool' churches and the great manor houses.

More latterly, the Cotswolds has come to represent elegance and wealth. In the C18, Bath and Cheltenham epitomised the elegance, hedonism and splendour of the Georgian era.

The landscape is rich in imagery: dry-stone walls divide the vast, sweeping sheep pastures and lazy, winding, trout streams meander through the rich pastureland. And, scattered across this landscape you will come across quaint hamlets undisturbed by coach, sightseer or time itself. All this makes for an idyllic scene rarely bettered in England.

In recent times this region's close proximity to London has attracted wealthy residents, and an increase in second homes bought by out-of-towners. This brings with it all the associated benefits and disadvantages. The region also attracts glitzy minor celebrities with their hangers on in tow, and the seemingly necessary trumpet and fanfare. This has opened the flood gates of more high-class restaurants and dining pubs which is a benefit to all (who can afford them).

The Circus, Bath

MAIN CENTRES

Bath. Is Bath the most beautiful city in England? Many believe so, for it is second only to London in the number of visitors it attracts. It will captivate you today as it has done so down the centuries, from the Romans to Jane Austen, to Robert Southey and the Romantic Poets, to the Rugby aficionados jostling to get into the Recreation Ground. There is surely only one way to see Bath (apart from the top of an open double-decker bus, or from a hot-air balloon) and that is to walk. So, prepare yourself, first with a good night's sleep, and second with a comfortable pair of shoes and a clear map. The day will be long and exhausting. Your eyes will be worn out with an overload of images, and your feet in need of a soothing bath. However, the next day you will be raring to go and see more of this visual feast and to revisit your favourite crescent. You have become a Bathophile. The Bath springs or hot waters were discovered by the mythical King Bladud (or Blaiddyd) in 863 BC, King of the Britons, and father of King Lear. The Celts venerated the site but it was the Romans in about 60-70 AD who developed the hot springs and built a wall around the 23 acre site naming it Aquae Sulis. The site held warm to hot, to very cold baths, sweating rooms, massage areas and fitness rooms. It prospered for 400 years until the Romans withdrew from Britain in 410 AD. In 973 the Abbey was chosen as the setting for the coronation of King Edgar, and in 1157 it received the seat of a Bishopric. The city saw much prosperity in the Middle Ages due to the sale of Cotswold wool. The building of today's Abbey started in the C15. But, the heyday of Bath began over

Burford's Gables Reflected

a 40-year period when three men of immense vision transformed the city with a populace of 3,000 into the Georgian city of 30,000 citizens. The three men were Beau Nash (Master of Ceremonies, manners and fashion), John Wood, (Architect), and Ralph Allen, (benefactor, financier and quarry owner who supplied the building materials). Today, Bath is an educational centre and host to many festivals: Literature, Music, Cricket, to name but a few. It is a bustling shopping centre with more than your average number of independent retailers. For those seeking refreshment there appears to be a café or bar on every corner, and it boasts some of the West Country's finest restaurants. For those arriving in a car, parking can be a nightmare. You can leave your car at Park-and- Ride near the Race Course at Lansdown on the northern side of the City, or purchase hourly tickets from most shops and take your chance. Beware of bus lanes. www.visitbath.co.uk

Bourton-On-The-Water. Love it, or hate it, this village attracts the crowds. It has been described as one of the most popular beauty spots in the Cotswolds, but one that invites mixed opinions. It can be charming on a quiet, frostbitten morning when only the postman is out and about, but is best avoided on a busy bank holiday when the hordes arrive in coaches and charabancs. With ice cream in hand the visitors sit beside the river wetting their bare feet in the Windrush, and not a stitch of green grass is visible through all the paraphernalia. The tourist brochures describe it as 'The Venice of the Cotswolds', no doubt because the River Windrush is spanned with low graceful bridges. You must, however, look beyond the crowds and the tacky gift shops and wander the little streets for there are some beautiful houses to admire. Bourton may not thrill the jaded teenager or hard-bitten traveller, but it will delight small children - mine loved to run across the little bridges, paddle in the river and feed the ducks, and you have, of course, Birdland, the Model Village, the Motoring Museum and the Model Railway, all devised for family fun and rainy days. The village is built above an underground reservoir. It is not an uncommon sight to see a sprightly pensioner move into the village, and within eighteen months, be seen wobbling along the lane, bent double by the damp. Bourton has its fair share of pubs that cater for the tourist. Perhaps the most traditional bar is in the Old New Inn. Tearooms are plentiful. July Carnival. Water Game - August bank holiday

Broadway. 'The Painted Lady of the Cotswolds' is a term often used to describe this village. The honey-coloured stone captivates the visitor today as it did in the C19 when William Morris and his pre-Raphaelite friends settled here. A slow walk up the High Street will unfold some large and impressive houses that have been homes to Edward Elgar, JM Barrie (Peter Pan), Ralph Vaughan Williams, Sir Gerald Navarro MP and Laura Ashley. These great houses with bow windows, dormers and finely graduated stone roofs are usually hidden behind statuesque gates. It has its fair share of hotels, restaurants, tearooms, art galleries and, a fine bookshop.

Burford. The first major Cotswold town you come to if travelling from the east, and what an Introduction. The wide High Street, with its classical Gables atop gracious houses, slopes down to the dreamy, River Windrush. Once, an important coach and wool centre bursting with activity, hostelries and dens of rumbustious entertainment. A history of civil rights and religious tolerance prevailed here with the Burford Levellers. On 17 May 1649, three soldiers were executed in Burford Churchyard on the orders of Oliver Cromwell. These three had sought to undermine the authority of Cromwell whom they considered to be a dictator, rather than a liberator. This event is celebrated every year with song, dance and speeches. Today, there are any number of inns, and pretty cottages hidden down the side streets. The churchyard is a quiet spot with decorated table tombs. The town has a wide selection of hotels, inns and tearooms and a couple of delis to make up lunchtime sandwiches. Feast of the Dragon and Street Fair in June.

Bourton-On-The-Water at Dawn

Lansdown Parade, Cheltenham

Cheltenham. A smaller version of Bath, often described as 'the most complete Regency town in England'. Elegant Regency buildings overlook the crescents, squares, tree-lined avenues and spacious parks. Cheltenham remains, in historic terms, a young town of a mere 300-years. It grew as a spa after George III had approved the waters in 1788. Thereafter, distinguished visitors such as George Handel and Samuel Johnson came to be revitalised. The Promenade is one of the most attractive shopping streets in England which becomes progressively more independent and up-market as you trudge with heavy bags and depleted purse west towards Montpelier. Style and fashion epitomise this smart town. Youth and hedonism, a-plenty. Cheltenham has seen a phenomenal explosion of new nightclubs, bars and restaurants patronised by the ever-increasing student population and, come the evening, by an influx of visitors from Birmingham, Bristol and Gloucester and, not least from the surrounding villages and small towns. It is no longer the home of Colonel Blimps and tweedy ladies of means. Cheltenham is proud of its calendar of festivals: Antique, Folk, Greenbelt, Jazz, Literature, Music, Science, Wychwood…but it is during the Cheltenham Festival of National Hunt Racing which takes place in March that the town takes on a carnival atmosphere. The Irish arrive in thousands and this brings out the Cheltonians hospitality. Hotel rooms are like gold dust so many of Cheltenham's citizens open their homes and do a brisk and highly profitable B&B trade for three or four nights. A centre of administration, commerce, education, high-tech industries and secret surveillance. The Countryside Commission and UCAS have their headquarters here. So do a number of large organisations. The University of Gloucestershire has expanded its faculties to countenance the weight of the highly regarded private schools. What stands out for those of us who arrive from the Gloucester side is the large circular building known as GCHQ, locally known as the Puzzle Palace. This was established after WWII as a secret surveillance centre for the Foreign Office. It is a most congenial town that could well be described as the centre for the Cotswolds. Its motto is: Salubritas et Eruditio 'Health and Education'. If you can achieve either of these then your luck is in.

Chipping Campden. If you chose to visit just one Cotswold village make sure it's this one. There is no better introduction. The harmony of Cotswold stone mirrors the town's prosperity in the Middle Ages. The Gabled Market Hall was built in 1627 by the wealthy landowner Sir Baptist Hicks whose mansion was burnt down in the Civil War, and the remains are the two lodges beside the Church. The Church of St James is a tall and statuesque 'Wool' church. William Grevel, one of the wealthiest wool merchants is remembered in the church on a brass transcription which reads: 'the flower of the wool merchants of all England'. Opposite Grevel's House is the Woolstaplers Hall, the meeting place for the fleece (staple) merchants. Dovers Cotswold Olympick Games & Scuttlebrook Wake, June.

Cirencester. One of the finest and most affluent towns in the Cotswolds lies surrounded by a plethora of attractive villages whose populace (often second home owners) tend to shop and hobnob in Ciren (as the locals call it). The smart shops and bars reflect the riches of its patrons. As the Roman town Corinium, it became the second largest Roman town (after London) in Britain. Its strategic position at the confluence of the major routes (the Fosse Way, Ermin Way and Akeman Street) combined with the vast rolling sheep pastures brought great wealth in the Middle Ages. The history of Cirencester and the Cotswolds is well documented at the impressive Corinium Museum. On the outskirts of the town stands the Royal Agricultural College, famous for producing generations of estate managers and farmers from all classes of society. All the best eating places appear to be on Black Jack Street. Monday and Friday are market days. July Carnival.

Market Hall, Chipping Campden

Moreton-In-Marsh. Perhaps the first Cotswold town you'll visit if coming from the north along the ancient Fosse Way. And, what an impressive site it is, too. The wide main street built by the Abbot of Westminster in 1220 for the sheep and arable sales is today a lively scene on market day, every Tuesday since King Charles I granted the town a Charter in 1637. But its origins go back to the Romans who built a military camp around 43-50 AD whilst planning the construction of the Fosse Way. It remains the largest town in the Central Wolds and is dominated by the Market Hall built in 1887 by Lord Redesdale, father of the Mitford sisters. Look out for the Curfew Tower, an unusual phenomenon on the corner of Oxford Street, dated 1633, which rang until 1860. A fine centre given to a number of inns, art galleries and independent retailers. Associated with the English Civil War, for the Royalist Cavalry was based here. Moreton (Agricultural & Horse) Show - 1st Saturday in September.

Cross Street, Cirencester

Stroud. This is not a pretty, pretty, almost too perfect Cotswold town. No. Stroud was as close to the dirt of the Industrial Revolution as any other town in the Gloucestershire Cotswolds. It has few architectural gems. However, its attraction lies in its energy and artistic ambitions (or pretensions). There has been a liberal, bohemian attitude at play here since the group of Tolstoyan Anarchists settled at Whiteways in 1898. There is a lively community of writers and artists living in the surrounding valleys. Many will have read Laurie Lee's Cider With Rosie about his early life in the Slad Valley but artists Michael Cardew, Lyn Chadwick and Norman Jewson settled here, too. And Damien Hirst has a business making up his prints and artworks in nearby Chalford. So, supposedly, the claim that it is the Arts and Crafts Centre of the Cotswolds, is justified. A busy café culture pervades, too. The weaving industry all began in a couple of cottages up the hill in Bisley (Jilly Cooper's domain), This moved into the town where 150 mills were soon in action using the water-powered valleys. But, as the C19 progressed much of this cloth- making moved north to the West Riding of Yorkshire. The surrounding valleys provide wonderful walks through combes and woodland that are so very different from the Central Wolds. Look out for the Subscription Rooms built around 1833. Fringe Festival - 2nd week of September. Arts Festival - October.

Kings Arms, Market Square, Stow On The Wold

Stow-On-The-Wold. With a name like this it is bound to attract visitors, and it has, and does so to this day, for with its exposed position at the intersection of eight roads (one being the Fosse Way) Stow has been party to some momentous events in history. The Romans used Stow as an encampment and route centre. The Viking merchants traded down the Fosse Way, but it was the Saxon hill farmers who laid the foundations for the fleece which created wealth for the wool merchants who used the great Market Place for sheep sales of 20,000, or more. It still has free parking and you may Wander freely about and admire the art galleries and the antique shops. More recently, the hostelries have been renovated and small hotels revitalized. For Stow has become a centre of Cotswold hospitality, again. But, wrap up before you climb that hill. 'Where the wind blows cold' so the song goes.

SMALLER CENTRES

Chipping Norton. A well situated hill-top town affording elegant spectacular views over the surrounding countryside. Mentioned in the Domesday Book. The new Market Place was built in 1205 and is today surrounded by elegant houses with Georgian facades. But it was the wool industry established in the C13 that brought wealth to this corner of Oxfordshire and, like so many before them and after, the wealthy merchants invested their coppers in the C15 'Wool' church in order to guarantee a place in heaven. The town's attraction is that it is very much a small market town responding to the demands of the local populace and is little affected by Cotswold tourism. It is home to some celebrities: Jeremy Clarkson, Susan Hill and, until his death, Ronnie Barker, who ran an antique emporium. Bookshop with coffee shop. Mop Fair in September.

Evesham. An attractive market town with tree-planted walks and lawns beside the River Avon. Centre for the Vale of Evesham's fruit growing industries. Abbey remains. Simon de Montfort, who fell at the Battle of Evesham in 1265, is buried in the churchyard. Almonry heritage Museum.

Malmesbury. Claims to be the oldest borough in England (although Barnstaple in North Devon may dispute this) - established in 880 AD. Military strategists have described its hilltop location as the best naturally defended inland position of all ancient settlements. No wonder then that King Athelstan, the first King of all England, chose it as his home. Set on the edge of the Cotswold escarpment, it is a cheaper place to stay than the more central towns. Its spirit though lies with the Wiltshire landscape. Dysons, the innovative design company of vacuum cleaners, is the major employer and has brought some much needed zest, style and money to this isolated town. However James Dyson was not the first inventor to work in the town. You must go back to the free-spirited monk, Eilmer, in the C11, who designed and built his own hang glider (see Malmesbury Abbey).

Nailsworth. In the last few years this little town has come alive! Transformed into a thriving, bustling shopping centre with bakery, restaurants, tearooms, arts and craft shops. An eclectic mix of Cotswold domestic and industrial architecture is to be seen dotted about the hillside overlooking a wooded valley. Its position is convenient as a centre for visiting Bath and the south Cotswolds.

Northleach. An attractive Cotswold village noted for its church and Market Place. Often overlooked because the A40 now bypasses the village which at first left it out on a limb. The village elders have done much to restore the lifeblood of this little community. It is worth a journey for the church, buildings and museums.

Tetbury. A market town with a fine church, St. Mary's. The town's recent claim to fame has been due to its proximity to Highgrove, Prince Charles' home at Doughton. The opening of his Highgrove shop on the High Street has brought a flux of visitors to the town with coaches bringing the traffic to a standstill. How this helps the rest of the town's merchants, one can only guess. Today, it is the Cotswold's centre for antiques. It has also had much welcome investment in the shape of new shops, galleries and places to eat and drink. The Woolsack Races on May Bank Holiday are fun to watch and cause great merriment if you are not forced to carry the heavy woolsack. Those with weak backs (or, common sense) are best left to be onlookers.

The Old Flour Mill, Tewkesbury

Market Hall, Tetbury

Tewkesbury. One of England's finest Medieval towns set at the confluence of the rivers Avon and Severn. Just look up at the gables of the many ancient buildings and admire (or venture into) one of the 30 narrow alleyways that make up this historic place so magnificently brought to life in John Moore's Brensham Trilogy. In the Middle Ages Tewkesbury was a flourishing centre of commerce: flour milling, mustard, brewing, malting and shipping. Today, it has its flourmills and is a centre for boating and tourism. It is still a busy market town of half-timbered buildings, overhanging upper storeys and carved doorways. Following the recent floods the town has a new energy and purpose. Note the new Tourist Information Centre and Out of the Hat Museum which symbolizes the ambition of this Town.

Winchcombe. This small town lies cradled in the Isbourne Valley. It was an ancient Saxon burh (small holding) and famous medieval centre visited from far and wide for the market, horse fair and monastery which was destroyed in the C16. You can still walk the narrow streets beside the C16 and C18 cottages, but do look up and admire the many fine gables above the shop fronts. There's a local saying: Were you born in Winchcombe? which is directed at those of us who leave doors open. It can be a wee bit drafty. For those who visit Sudeley Castle give yourself some time to explore here.

Witney. The largest shopping centre in West Oxfordshire, and a dormitory town to Oxford that has seen rapid expansion in the last 20 years. A town of hustle and bustle, with a good share of attractive limestone buildings. Note the C17 Butter Cross with gabled roof, clock turret and sundial, the Town Hall with room overhanging a piazza and across Church Green the unusually handsome spire to the Parish Church, visible from far and wide. Witney has a fair compliment of ancient hostelries and the Angel Inn overlooking Church Green is steeped in history. Ethnic restaurants are plentiful and diverse in their culinary

arts. There have been signs of Iron Age and Roman settlements but the first records of any activity date from 969 AD. The Bishop of Westminster built a palace in 1044 which was eventually excavated in 1984. In 1277 the town's business centred on the fulling and cloth mills. In the Middle Ages gloves, blankets and brewing were the staple industries. Earlys of Witney, the blanket makers were in business for 300 years until quite recently. All of this has been ably recorded in the local Cogges Manor Countryside Museum.

Woodstock. A pretty town of stone built houses, interesting shops and smart hotels, and a practical centre for exploring the eastern Cotswolds and Oxford. Famous for glove-making in the C16, and for Blenheim Palace (great walks), the birthplace of Sir Winston Churchill (1874-1965) who is buried in nearby Bladon churchyard. There area number of antique shops, art galleries and a fascinating museum plus a melee of delis, inns, restaurants, tearooms and coffee shops.

Italian Gardens, Blenheim Palace

You may also like to consider:

Wotton-Under-Edge. As the name suggests, Wotton hangs on the southern edge of the Cotswold escarpment. In its long history, the Berkeley family have dominated the town with varying success. King John's mercenaries devastated the Berkeley's property in the C11. Later, the simmering dispute between the de Lisles and the Berkeleys was sorted out in the latter's favour at the Battle at Nibley Green in 1470. The Berkeleys were generous patrons; Katherine Lady Berkeley established one of the country's first grammar schools here in 1384. Weaving and cloth making grew from cottage industries in the C13. Wotton is quiet market town with some splendid C17 and C18 buildings. The countryside (The Bottoms) to the north of the town is quite outstanding, and popular with walkers. Isaac Pitman, 1813-97, who invented shorthand lived on Orchard Street. The Ram Inn is probably the town's oldest building but, it is to St Mary the Virgin that all historians will be drawn.

Arlington Row, Bibury

SCENIC VILLAGES

Bibury. Described by William Morris as one of the prettiest villages in England, and few would argue with him. It attracts the crowds and is thus the stop-off point for many coach tours. It is a honey-pot village made up of rose-covered cottages set behind idyllic kitchen gardens, and all overlook the sleepy River Coln inhabited by swans, trout and duckling. During the C17 Bibury was notorious as a buccaneering centre for gambling and horse racing.

Castle Combe. Is this a soulless Hollywood film set once visited by thousands of Japanese and US tourists, or is it one of the prettiest villages in the south Cotswolds lieing sheltered in a hidden valley surrounded by steep, wooded hills? Given the recent demise of American and Japanese coach parties, the post office and gift shops have closed. It is a museum piece more recently used for the film War Horse. In former times, an important medieval, wool centre evidenced by the weavers and clothiers' cottages that descend from the Market Cross to By Brook, and the three-arch bridge. There is parking at the top and bottom end of the village.   www.castle-combe.com

Duntisbournes, The. A group of isolated hamlets dotted along a beautiful wooded valley. Duntisbourne Abbot stands at the head of the valley. the Dunt Brook flows through each hamlet. The road to Duntisbourne Leer runs adjacent to the stream. Middle Duntisbourne and Duntisbourne Rouse are two farming hamlets, the latter famous for its idyllic Saxon Church.

Eastleach. The twin hamlets of Eastleach Turville and Eastleach Martin face each other across the River Leach. The ancient clapper bridge (Keble's Bridge) connects the two and was built by the Keble family whose descendant, John Keble, was curate here in 1815. He founded the Oxford Movement, and is know for his volume of religious verse The Christian Year. In spring, hundreds of daffodils grow on both banks, and hidden behind the trees is the Norman Church of St Michael and St Martin. Across the river the tiny church of St Andrews. Traditional village hostelry, the Victoria Inn.

Great Tew. A sensationally beautiful village lined with ironstone cottages covered in thatch and stone tiles. Much of the village was designed by the Scottish architect, John Claudius London. The Falkland Arms is named after Lord Falkland who lived here, and who died fighting for Charles I at the Battle of Newbury.

Great Tew, Oxon

Guiting Power. A hidden, somnolent estate village that surprisingly manages to support two pubs, a village shop and bakery, a nursery school and an active village hall. The blue-grey cottages belong to the Cochrane Estate (or Guiting Manor Amenity Trust) that has thankfully saved this village from greedy developers and second homers. The Church of St Michael & All Angels lies on the edge of the village and has some Norman features, a beautiful Tympanum and some weather-beaten tombstones. It was an early Anglo-Saxon settlement called Gyting Broc. A classical and jazz music festival is held in late July for the past 38 years and attracts many artists of international renown. www.guitingfestival.org

Naunton. A pretty village surrounded by rolling sheep pastures and overlooked by some steep gallops. The handsome Church has some interesting gargoyles and a stone pulpit

Painswick. Its local description as 'The Queen of the Cotswolds' is justified. The houses and cottages are built from a grey, almost white limestone, in marked contrast to Broadway and Chipping Campden, and some of the buildings have a Palladian, statuesque dignity about them. Look out for the Court House and the Cotswolds88hotel. Wander down the pretty side streets and visit the churchyard famous for the legendary 99 yew trees. The 100th yew tree has been planted time and again, but has never survived. Painswick is one of the gems of the south Cotswolds, and is a worthy base from which to explore this region. It is also connected to a network of footpaths including the Cotswold Way so you can arrive by car or taxi and then just walk for the rest of your stay.

Slaughters, The. Lower Slaughter is one of the most popular villages in the Cotswolds. Little bridges cross the Eye Stream which runs beside rows of golden cottages. The much painted C19 redbrick Corn Mill stands on the western edge of the village. Upper Slaughter is a couple of miles upstream and has an old Manor House once lived in by the Slaughter family, an old Post Office with a beautiful kitchen garden and, along a lane past the church, a ford crosses the stream hidden beneath lush greenery.

Stanton & Stanway. A charming village with houses of warm honey-coloured stone restored by Sir Philip Scott, 1903-37. Centre for equine excellence in the Vine, a popular horse riding centre. The Mount Inn is a welcome refuge if one's tackling the Cotswold Way. Stanway is dominated by the outstanding Manor House. In its grounds, one of the country's finest tithe barns designed with the Golden Proportion in mind, and across the road, a thatched cricket pavilion, set on staddle stones. The beautiful Gatehouse is C17, and was probably built by Timothy Strong of Little Barrington. It bears the arms of the Tracy family. The little Church of St Peter has C14 origins and some amusing gargoyles.

You may also like to consider:

Bisley, Coln Dennis, Coln Rogers, Coln St Aldwyns, Frampton-On-Severn, Minster Lovel, Sapperton, Sheepscombe, Sherborne, Slad, The Ampneys, The Barringtons, The Swells, The Wychwoods…to name a few.

Lower Slaughter

Stanway in winter

Barrow Wake, Birdlip Hill

PREHISTORIC SITES

Bagendon Earthworks, Cirencester. Remains of the Dobunni tribes' headquarters which was the capital of the Cotswolds in the C1 AD. The settlement was abandoned ten years after the Roman Conquest. Iron Age silver coins excavated here.

Barrow Wake, Birdlip. Deep scarp edge. Favourite viewpoint. Roman pottery found at the bottom of scarp. Car park.

Belas Knap Long Barrow, Winchcombe. In Old English translates 'beacon mound'. A burial chamber, 4,000 years old. Opened in 1863 to reveal 38 skeletons. In superb condition and good viewpoint. Steep footpath from road.

Bredon Hill Fort, Nr Tewkesbury. Iron Age fort with two ramparts and scene of great battle at time of Christ, possibly against the Belgic invaders. The hacked remains of 50 men were found near entrance.

Superb views over to Wales, Vale of Evesham, the rivers Severn and Avon, and to the Cotswolds.

Grim's Ditch, Blenheim. Disconnected series of ditches and banks built by Iron Age tribes (Belgic) to defend their grazing enclosures. Best sections in Blenheim and Ditchley Parks. Grim is one of the names of Woden – the masked one, the god of victory, death and magic power, the high god of the Anglo-Saxons before their conversion to Christianity in the C7.

Hetty Pegler's Tump Uley Tumulus, Nr Uley. Neolithic Long Barrow 120ft x 22ft, 4 chambers, 38 skeletons found in C19. Torch and Wellington boots needed.

Uley Bury Iron Age Hill Fort. This is the Cotswolds most famous Iron Age site. The deep ramparts provide superb views across the Severn Vale, Welsh Hills, Dursley and Owlpen Woods. It's an enclosed area of about 32 acres and is

Belas Knapp Long Barrow, Winchcombe

Uley Bury & Cam Long Down

used for arable crops. Of more interest, it has an easy circular walk possible for large wheeled pushchairs.

Meon Hill, Mickleton. Iron-age hillfort. The locals keep well away from this spot for fear of the spookery of witchcraft.

Nan Tow's Tump, Nr Leighterton. A Long Barrow. 9ft high and 100ft in Diameter crowned with trees. Believed to contain skeleton of Nan Tow, a local Witch buried upright.

Rollright Stones, Nr Chipping Norton. The King's Men is a Bronze Age stone circle 100 feet in diameter, 2,000-1,800 BC and is easily accessible from the road. Just 400 yards east of this circle are The Whispering Knights, remains of a Bronze Age burial chamber. And, isolated in a field, the King's Stone.

Carving of Roman Figures, Corinium Museum, Cirencester

ROMAN SITES

Akeman Street. Roman road built to provide communications between military units and their forts. Best seen near Coln St Aldwyn and Quenington.

Chedworth Roman Villa (NT). Discovered in 1864 by a local gamekeeper and later excavated between 1864 and 1866 revealing remains of a Romano-British villa containing mosaics, baths and hypocausts. Family trails. Museum. Open daily (except Ms Mar to mid-Nov) from 10. 01242 890256 www.nationaltrust.org.uk

Corinium Dobunorum. The second Largest Roman town after London Londinium. Amphitheatre on Querns Hill and villas hereabouts. See the Corinium Museum for details.

Ermin Way. Roman road linking Cirencester with Gloucester and Kingsholm; two encampments on the edge of Roman civilisation. Built and manned by troops. This undulating road still leaves a marked pattern across the landscape.

Fosse Way. The famous Roman road linking Exeter with Lincoln that runs diagonally across the Cotswold escarpment. One can still see evidence of Staging Posts and Bakehouses beside the road.

North Leigh Roman Villa (EH), Nr Woodstock. This ruin was excavated in 1813 and 60 rooms were revealed surrounding the courtyard with a beautiful mosaic pavement. A charming spot beside the River Evenlode. Open daily in summer.

Salmonsbury Camp, Bourton-On-The-Water. The Romans' second legion of 5,000 soldiers was encamped here and built Lansdown Bridge to ford the Windrush on the Fosse Way.

Spoonley Roman Villa, Nr Winchcombe. Excavated in 1882. What few remains there are, are not clearly visible. The site lies on private property with a footpath passing, nearby.

Witcombe Roman Villa (EH), Nr Gloucester. Discovered by workmen whilst removing an ash tree. Later, excavated In 1818, and 1935. Dates from C1 AD, and occupied until the C4. Tessellated Pavements, mosaics and Bath Wing. Closed to view.

Wortley Roman Villa, Nr Wotton. Believed to be in existence from the C1 to C4. It was accidentally discovered in 1981 when an archaeological dig by the University of Keele unveiled Roman and Saxon coins, painted wall plaster, pottery and a damaged hypocaust.Much is now on display in Stroud Museum.

You may also like to consider:

Woodchester Roman Villa. This huge villa was excavated by Lysons in 1993 and revealed 64 rooms including the Orpheus Pavement. Today, there is little to see. The pavement lies buried and plans to uncover it lie dormant.

Mosaic of Spring, Chedworth Roman Villa

Bath Abbey, Bath

ABBEYS & CATHEDRALS

Bath Abbey. The Church of St Peter and St Paul has seen three churches occupy this site: an Anglo-Saxon church in 757 and a Norman Cathedral in 1090 but later in 1137 much of this was destroyed by fire. Today's building was founded in 1499 to replace the ruin damaged in the fire. But, it had again to be rebuilt in 1611 following Henry VIII's Dissolution of the Monasteries. In simple architectural terms it can be described as Perpendicular Gothic and cruciform in plan. The fan vaulting of the Nave is very fine and was designed by Robert and William Vertue designers of Henry VII's chapel in Westminster Abbey. It was never finished until Gilbert Scott completed the original designs in the 1860s. Note the Stairway to Heaven on the West Front: two ladders of carved angels are climbing towards Christ. Tower Tours. Open daily. 01225 422462 www.bathabbey.org

Bruern Abbey, Nr Bledington. The present building, a school, was built on the site of a Cistercian abbey established in 1147, and dissolved in 1536. A vaulted chamber is all that remains (within a Georgian cottage) in the grounds.

Cirencester Abbey. Only the Abbey grounds remain. A peaceful enclave behind the Parish Church of St John the Baptist. Open daily.

Gloucester Cathedral. The Cathedral Church of St Peter and the Holy and Undivided Trinity. Without exception the most magnificent building in Gloucestershire and one of the finest of all English cathedrals. The building's foundation stone was laid down by Abbot Serlo in 1089 on the site of a religious house founded by Osric, an Anglo-Saxon prince living here in about 678-9 AD. The Nave was completed in 1130. Its architecture is Romanesque, with some early Perpendicular. The reconstruction of the Quire followed the burial in 1327 of Edward II. The East Window behind the altar had at its installation the largest display of medieval stained glass in the world and dates from 1350. The same year, fan vaulting was invented here at Gloucester and its intricate design covers the roof of the cloisters. Some would argue that Gloucester also saw the birth of Perpendicular architecture. In the South Transept survives the oldest of all Perpendicular windows. Allow a couple of hours to wander around this spiritual hot house. There are tours of the crypt and tower. You will also be shown the location used for part of Hogwarts in the Harry Potter films. Evensong is a most magical experience not to be missed, as is the Christmas Carol service. Restaurant. Open daily 7.30am to 6pm. 01452 528095 www.gloucestercathedral.org.uk

Hailes Abbey (EH/NT). Built in 1246 by Richard, Earl of Cornwall, brother of Henry III, having vowed he would found a religious house if he survived a storm at sea. Museum. The abbey became a popular place of pilgrimage in the Middle Ages until Henry VIII closed it down. It remains an attractive ruin with many surviving artifacts on display in the museum. Open daily Apr to Oct 31 10-dusk. 01242 602398 www.nationaltrust.org.uk

Malmesbury Abbey & Churchyard, Malmesbury

Tewkesbury Abbey in Flood, Glos

Kingswood Abbey Gatehouse (EH), Nr Wotton-Under-Edge. The few remains of a C16 Cistercian abbey dissolved in 1538.

Malmesbury Abbey Church of St Peter & St Paul. Founded as a Benedictine Monastery in 676 AD by the saintly and scholarly Brother Aldhelm. King Athelstan was buried here in 941 AD. By the C11 the monastery held the second largest library in Europe and was a place of learning and pilgrimage. The Abbey was built and completed by 1180. The tall spire rose to 431 feet (131m) and was to be seen for miles around. However, in 1500 it collapsed destroying the Nave and the Transept. A few years later, in 1550, the West Tower also collapsed. What you see today is less than half of the original structure. Yet it still remains a formidable church, and a sight to behold. It was also a place of great inspiration for in 1010 the monk Eilmer of Malmesbury became the first man to fly by jumping off the roof of the Tower and flying his hang glider 200 yards before crashing and breaking both his legs – Leonardo da Vinci was to design a similar machine 350 years later. Open daily 10-5 (-4 winter).
www.malmesburyabbey.com

Pershore Abbey. Established in the late C10 by Benedictines. C14 tower and the superb vaulting of the Presbytery, remain. Beautiful Early English Choir, but sadly much was destroyed by Henry VIII. Visitor Centre summer weekends. Look out for the intricate wooden sculpture in the grounds. Open daily 9-4.30 (-3.30 winter).01386 552071
www.pershoreabbey.fsnet.co.uk

Prinknash Abbey. Benedictine Monastery with C14 and C15 origins set amidst an idyllic rolling landscape. Abbey church opens 8-5. Monastery garden with possible Tudor origins. Café/shop opens W-Su 10-4. Grounds open daily. 01452 812455
www.prinknashabbey.org.uk

Tewkesbury Abbey. Founded in 1087 by the nobleman Robert Fitzhamon. However, the present building was started in 1102 to house Benedictine monks. The Norman abbey was consecrated in 1121. The Nave and roof finished in the C14 in the Decorated style. Much is Early English and Perpendicular, although it is larger than many cathedrals and has according to Pevsner 'the finest Romanesque Tower in England'. The Abbey opens its doors to three major music festivals: Musica Deo Sacra, the Three Choirs Festival and the Cheltenham Music Festival. You can park opposite and take a tour. Info on 01684 850959. Shop and refectory. Open daily 8.30am to 5.30pm.
www.tewkesburyabbey.org.uk

Pershore Abbey

St John the Baptist, Burford

GREAT CHURCHES

Adderbury, St Mary. Early C13 cruciform. C14 West tower with massive carvings. Superb chancel and vestry.

Bloxham, St Mary. C14 spire. Carvings. C15 wall paintings. East window by William Morris and Edward Burne-Jones.

Burford, St John the Baptist. One of the great Cotswold churches built in the C15 with proceeds earned by the local wool merchants. Hence, the term 'Wool' church. It has a spacious interior more akin to a small cathedral. The porch and spire c.1450 are outstanding, as are the sculptured table tombs in the churchyard. Inside, don't miss the intricate medieval stained glass and the monuments (painted figures). Open daily 9-5 except during services.

Chipping Campden, St James. A fine old 'Wool' church, of Norman origin, restored in the C15; with a tall and elegant tower and large Perpendicular nave. 'Brilliant' in late summer afternoons. C15 Cope, and a unique pair of C15 Altar Hangings. Brasses of Woolstaplers. C15 Falcon Lecturn. Open daily from 10.

St James', Chipping Campden

Fairford Church Stained Glass

St John the Baptist, Cirencester

Cirencester, St John the Baptist. A fine mix of the C14 and C15, the largest of the 'Wool' churches, and the easiest to recognize with its three-storied, fan-vaulted porch. The porch, formerly the Town Hall, overshadows the Market Place. C15 'wine glass' pulpit, Ann Boleyn Cup, and many fine brasses. Open M-Sa 9.30-5, Su in winter 2.15-5.30, in summer 12.30-6.

Fairford, St Mary the Virgin. The perfect, late C15 Perpendicular church that is world-famous for the outstanding 28 stained glass windows depicting scenes from Genesis to the Last Judgement. Of further interest are the carved misericords and recumbent brasses. Open 9.30-5.30 for visits and guided tours. 01285 712611

Highnam, Holy Innocents. A Masterpiece of Victorian design, and Thomas Parry's monument to his beloved, Isabella. Henry Woodyer (disciple of Pugin), Hardman and Parry completed this in 1851 with no expense spared; Wall paintings dominate the Nave, the floor with Minton tiles, the exterior with crockets and pinnacles. Open weekends.

Northleach, St Peter & St Paul. C15. The South Porch has been described as the most lovely in all England: Tall pinnacles and statue filled niches. From afar, the church appears to hover above the town. Brasses of wealthy wool barons. Guided tours: 01451 861172.

Painswick, St Mary. It is the soaring spire that will first captivate you, then as you enter, it will be the line of yew trees and then, as you wander around the churchyard, the tombs or monuments carved with their intricate figures. But, do look up and admire the gold clock. The spire has been struck by lightning on many occasions, in 1763 and 1883. The 100th yew tree always fades away.

Winchcombe, St Peter. One of the great 'Wool' churches. It is of a C15 Perpendicular design but is strangely plain, yet dignified. Not as elaborate as some of the other 'Wool' churches. For example, it has no chancel arch. The gargoyles are the one notable feature, and a circumnavigation of the exterior is advised. The weathercock is the County's finest.

Painswick Church

St Mary's Parish Church, Bibury

SMALLER CHURCHES

Ampney Crucis. C14 wall paintings. Saxon, Early Norman and Perpendicular features. Life-size effigies. Jacobean pews.

Berkeley, St Mary. One of Gloucestershire's most historic and interesting churches with a mass of features: Ring of ten bells, Norman doorway, C12 font, C13 chancel, C13-15 murals, C15 rood screen, C16 brass, Berkeley family tombs from the C15, and life-size effigies in alabaster, Jenner family vault and separate Gothic tower built in 1753. www.stmarys-berkeley.co.uk

Bibury, St Mary. If you seek a refuge from the hurly burly of Bibury's tourists then walk along the banks of the River Coln and you'll soon find the entrance to this pretty church. With evidence of Saxon remains, Norman font and superb sculptured table tombs.

Broadway, St Eadburgh's. A rare architectural gem of almost perfect proportions with a mix of C12-C18 additions. Superb brass work, topiary in churchyard, interesting tombstones and a welcome retreat from the hustle and bustle of Broadway.

Buckland, St Michaels. An exquisite church preserved with an almost undisturbed history from the C13 to the C17. Beautiful roof: painted and wood-panelled. C14 tower with gargoyles. C15 stained glass in East window restored by William Morris. Not to be missed, the Wainscotting: medieval wooden benches along the far wall as you enter. The Hazel Bowl made in 1607 of Dutch maple with a silver rim. The Buckland Pall, C15 embroidered vestments from the V & A Museum, London. Sadly, the medieval frescoes were removed by the restorer FS Waller in 1885.

Deerhurst (Odda's Chapel). One of the few surviving Saxon chapels left in England. Earl Odda dedicated this rare chapel to the Holy Trinity on the 12th April 1056 in memory of his brother. Open daily.

Eastleach; Church of St Michael & St Martin. Founded by Richard Fitzpons, one of William the Conqueror's Knights. It has a C14 North transept, decorated windows and, a memorable exterior beside the river fronted by daffodils in spring. It closed for services in 1982, and the Church of St Andrews. Hidden beneath the trees this tiny church has a more interesting interior than its neighbour. Note the splendid C14 saddleback-tower of a Transitional and Early English period style. A Norman doorway c.1130 with a carved Tympanum of Christ

St Eadburgh's Churchyard, Broadway

Swinbrook. Fettiplace monuments. Mitford family memorials.

Kelmscott. Wall painting. William Morris tomb by Philip Webb.

Wotton-Under-Edge, St Mary the Virgin. The first church on this site was probably destroyed by King John's mercenaries in the C11. The present structure was consecrated in 1283. Its Perpendicular tower, one of the county's finest has corner buttresses crowned with crocketed pinnacles. The marble tomb and the C15 brasses of Thomas, Lord Berkeley and his wife are outstanding. Note the C16 stained glass. Edward Barnsley in the Gimson tradition (Arts & Crafts Movement) designed the new altar and reredos on the north wall. The organ originally came from St. Martin in the Fields and had been a gift from George 1. George Handel played on it. Yet, the church lacks the beauty of Burford or Chipping Campden and can not be described as a notable "Wool" church.

Bredon Tithe Barn, Bredon

ESTATE & TITHE BARNS

Bredon Barn (NT). A beautifully constructed large medieval threshing barn extending to 132 feet. Expertly restored after fire. Open mid-Mar to end Oct W Th & W/Es 10-6 (Dusk). 01451 844257 www.nationaltrust.org.uk

Doughton Tithe Barn. Just across the road from Highgrove. This lies in the grounds of what I consider to be one of the most enchanting, unusual and beautiful of the Cotswolds many outstanding buildings. A VW Camper Van often peers through the doorway.

Enstone Tithe Barn, Rectory Farm. Dates from 1382 and is built with some magnificent timbers.

Frocester Court's Medieval Estate Barn. This is an enormous barn built between 1284 and 1306. It remains the second largest in England, and is one of the best preserved, with massive oak roof and is used every day by the farmer who owns it. For conducted tours (of 5 or more) phone 01453 823250.

Great Barn, Great Coxwell (NT). This quite magnificent C13 building provided income to Beaulieu Abbey. A favourite of William Morris who described it "unapproachable in its dignity". Open daily dawn to dusk. 01793 762209

Middle Littleton Tithe Barn (NT). This C13 barn is considered one of the finest in the country with ten bays and 130 feet long. Open daily Apr to Oct 2-5. 01905 371006 www.nationaltrust.org.uk

Postlip Hall & Tithe Barn. A former Jacobean Manor House set in fifteen acres, Postlip Hall has been for the past 40 years a co-housing idyll. Eight families live in separate dwellings, working the organic kitchen garden and grounds, and pursuing their own creative pleasures, be it writing, painting, sculpting or inventing. The original tithe barn is also in continual use except when it is hired out as a venue for weddings, parties and beer festivals

Southam Tithe Barn. C14 or C15 with 8-bays and in need of renovation. I remember it well, the venue for my 21st Party.

Stanway Tithe Barn. This was designed in the C14 for Tewkesbury Abbey with the Golden Proportion in mind. It stands beside a pond in the grounds of the Manor House.

Swalcliffe Barn. Early C15 tithe barn with fascinating displays of Oxfordshire's agricultural and trade vehicles. Exhibition of 2,500 years of the area. Open East Su to Oct Su & BH Ms 2-5. 01295 788278

< *Berkeley Family Tomb, Berkeley Church*

Sudeley Castle, Winchcombe

Berkeley Castle

HISTORIC BUILDINGS

Arlington Row, Bibury (NT). These Iconic cottages were originally monastic wool barns. However, in the C17 they were converted into weavers' homes. Now domestic dwellings, they overlook Rack Isle, a four-acre water meadow where cloth was once hung out to dry.

Badminton House. The home of the Dukes of Beaufort and venue for the annual Badminton Horse Trials. The estate was bought by the Worcesters in 1682. It was the 3rd Duke who was responsible for the house as we see it today. First, he invited James Gibbs to set about remodelling the East and West wings, then William Kent finished the North Front in the Palladian style. Fox hunting has been a great passion of the Beauforts. Their early forebears hunted all the way to London and back. Publishing was another passion. From 1885 to 1902 they devised The Badminton Library of Sports & Pastimes - an aristocratic leather bound series of books that was like a combination of Punch and your High Street cricket or football magazine, albeit a little more high brow. And, of course, the game of Badminton was reintroduced here in 1873 following its Indian origins. The house is closed to the public. The closest you'll get is to visit during the Three Day Horse Trials.

Berkeley Castle. Home of the Berkeley family for the last 850 years. It remains a splendidly preserved Norman fortress with an enclosing curtain wall. Scene of Edward II's murder in 1327. Lovely terraced gardens. Superb Butterfly House. Open East to Oct Su-Th 11-5.30. 01453 810332 www.berkeley-castle.com

Blenheim Palace. The home of the Dukes of Marlborough was built as Queen Anne's gift to John Churchill, 1st Duke of Marlborough, for his defeat of Louis XIV in 1704, 'a monument to commemorate a military victory, and to glorify the Queen'. It is considered to be Vanburgh's C18 baroque masterpiece, although much of the detail was by Nicholas Hawksmoor. There are fine paintings, a Churchill Exhibition, tapestries, a 10,000 volume library and parkland designed by 'Capability' Brown. Plus, other attractions: the Butterfly House, Marlborough Maze, Adventure Play Area and Herb Garden. Restaurant. Palace open from mid-Feb to mid-Dec, daily to 2 Nov, then W-Su 10.30-5.30 (last admission 4.45pm), Park open daily all year (9-5) for rambling and dog walking. 0800 84965500 www.blenheimpalace.com

Buscot Park (NT). C18 house with park and superb water garden designed by Harold Peto. Collection of art: Italian, Dutch, Flemish, Spanish and English Schools. Chinese porcelain. Tea room. Open Apr to Sept W Th & F (including Good F, East W/Es) 2-6, and alternate W/Es in each month 2-6. Grounds also M & Tu 2-6. 01367 240786 www.buscot-park.com

Charlton Park. Palatial mansion built in 1607. Home to the Earls of Suffolk since the C16. There are 4,500 acres of arable and woodland with trout fishing and game shooting on hand. It is also the venue for WOMAD, the World of Music, Arts & Dance festival, with its own park and camp facility. 01666 822146
www.charltonpark.co.uk

Cheltenham, Pittville Pump Room. A masterpiece of C19 Greek Revivalism adorned with colonnaded facades, portico, pillared and balconied hall. Open daily, except during private functions. 01242 264231
www.pittvillepumproom.org.uk

Chipping Norton, Bliss Tweed Mill. Built by William Bliss in 1872 to house his textile factory. He was instrumental in encouraging the railways to reach Chipping Norton. The mill closed as a factory in 1980 and was converted into domestic apartments. It is still quite a sight from the road and was, apparently, one of Sir John Betjeman's favourite buildings.

Dyrham Park (NT). C17 William and Mary mansion house set in a deer park with elegant formal gardens. The house belonged to the family of Sir William Blathwayt's wife, Mary Wynter. Blathwayt was secretary of war to William III (1671-1720). Sir William started to remodel the dilapidated Tudor mansion on site in 1692-1699. Victorian domestic quarters, Splendid collection of Dutch paintings. Film location for 'Remains of the Day' (1993). Open mid-March to 2 Nov daily except W & Th 11-5. Park open all year. 0117 9372501
www.nationaltrust.org.uk

Farnborough Hall (NT). A beautiful honey-coloured stone house sits in parkland created in the 1740s. Noted for the exquisite C18 plasterwork. Parkland walks and lake views. Open Apr to Sept, W & Sa, 2-5.30. 01295 690002
www.nationaltrust.org.uk

You may also like to consider:

Frampton Court. A Grade I Vanbrugh House, garden and family home. Fine panelling, original furniture and porcelain,1732. Superb Gothic C18 garden building, The Orangery for self-catering accommodation (sleeps 8). B&B. Fine landscaping with park, lake and ornamental canal. Home of the 'The Frampton Flora' a famous wild flower painting. C16 Wool Barn for hire. Country fair in September. 01452 740698
www.framptoncourtestate.co.uk

Lodge Park (NT). A 'little' property with a big (boozy) history. A grandstand (folly) built by John 'Crump' Dutton in 1634 so he could watch deer coursing in comfort and share his passion for gambling, drinking and entertaining with his friends. Open mid Mar to Oct, F & W/Es, 11-4. 01451 844130
www.nationaltrust.org.uk

Sezincote House & Garden. House designed in the Indian style (and inspiration for the Brighton Pavilion) is beautifully set in an oriental water garden. House open May to Sept, Th F & BH Ms 2.30-5.30. Garden open Jan to Nov Th F & BH Ms 2-6. 01386 700444
www.sezincote.co.uk

Sudeley Castle. A Tudor house and the original home of the Seymour family. Katherine Parr, widow of Henry VIII lived here and lies buried in the chapel. There is a fine collection of needlework, furniture and tapestries plus paintings by Van Dyck, Rubens and Turner. All surrounded by award-winning gardens and open parkland. The Castle is open daily Apr to Oct 10.30-5. 01242 602308
www.sudeleycastle.co.uk

Upton House & Gardens (NT). This house exhibits the lifestyle of a 1930s millionaire. It also has an outstanding display of English and Continental Old Masters paintings plus a wealth of herbaceous borders, terraces and tranquil water gardens. Open most days. See website for details. 01295 670266
www.nationaltrust.org.uk

Woodchester Mansion. Be prepared for a good 1-mile walk from the car park down to this unfinished masterpiece of Victorian stone masonry set in a secret Cotswold valley. The restoration project is on-going and ambitious. Bat Exhibition. Open East-Oct most W/Es 11-5. 01453 861541
www.woodchestermansion.org.uk

Dyrham Park, Bath

Broughton Castle

MANOR HOUSES

Broughton Castle. Moated medieval manor house, substantially enlarged in the C16. Magnificent plaster ceilings, fine panelling and fireplaces. Interesting Civil War connections. In the family of the Lords Saye and Sele for over 600 years. Multi-coloured borders. The location for much of the film, Shakespeare in Love. Open East & BHs, then W & Su May to mid-Sept, also Th in July & Aug 2-5. 01295 276070 www.broughtoncastle.com

Chavenage. A haunted Elizabethan manor house that has remained virtually unchanged for 400 years. Aeplica of a bygone age. It contains two complete tapestry rooms, furniture and relics of the Civil War. Guided tours by the family. Specialises in weddings and corporate events. Open East Su & M, also May to Oct Th, Su & BHs 2-5. 01666 502329 www.chavenage.com

Frampton Manor. Grade I timber framed medieval Manor House with walled garden and barn. C12 Birthplace of 'Fair Rosamund' Clifford, mistress to Henry II. House and garden open by written appointment for groups of 10 or more. Tours: 01452 740268.

Kelmscott Manor. The Elizabethan home of William Morris, the C19 poet, craftsman and socialist. Houses his furnishings which can be identified as examples from the Arts & Crafts Movement. Paintings by his fellow pre-Raphaelite, Dante Gabriel Rossetti. Open Apr to Oct W & Sa 11-5, Group visits on Th by arrangement. 01367 252486 www.kelmscottmanor.co.uk

Kingston Bagpuize House. A beautiful early C18 manor house in parkland setting. The garden contains shrubs, bulbs and herbaceous borders. Teas. Small gift shop. Open mid-May to mid-July M-Tu 1-6, Su 11-2. Gardens open more frequently. See website or phone for details. 01865 820259 www.kingstonbagpuizehouse.org.uk

Owlpen Manor. An iconic group of picturesque Cotswold buildings: Manor House, Tithe Barn, Church, Mill and Court House. Water Garden and terrace. The Tudor manor dates from 1450 to 1616 but the whole estate has 900 years

Owlpen Manor & Church, Uley

Snowshill Manor

of history to impart. Special Group Visits, & Weddings. Cottages for hire.   01453 860261
www.owlpen.com

Rodmarton Manor. This is a unique building built by Ernest Barnsley and his Cotswold group of craftsmen for the Biddulph family from 1909 to 1929. It displays Cotswold "Arts and Crafts" furniture, metalwork and wall hangings. The 8-acre garden is a series of outdoor rooms and is a marvel throughout the year. Refreshments. Open East M, then May to Sept W, Sa & BHs 2-5. 01285 841253
www.rodmarton-manor.co.uk

Snowshill Manor & Garden (NT). A Cotswold manor house containing Charles Paget Wade's extraordinary collection of craftsmanship, and design, amounting to some 22,000 items; from toys to musical instruments, Samurai armour to clocks and bicycles. Open mid-Mar to Oct W-Su 12-5, grounds, restaurant and shop from 11.   01386 852410
www.nationaltrust.org.uk

Stanton Harcourt Manor House & Gardens. A unique collection of medieval buildings. The house contains fine pictures, silver, furniture and porcelain. Moat and stew ponds. Pope's Tower. Open Apr-Sept as advertised. 01865 881928

Stanway House & Water Garden. This exquisite Jacobean Manor House and Gatehouse is built from the local stone known as Guiting

Yellow which lights up when the sun touches it. All is set within an enchanting and ancient parkland designed by a numerologist, the home of the Earl of Wemyss and March. The partially restored C18 Cascade and Canal was designed by the highly respected Charles Bridgman, and is now open June to Aug, Tu & Th 2-5. 01386 584469
www.stanwayfountain.co.uk

You may also like to consider:

Compton Wynyates. A Tudor dream house built 1460 with multi-coloured bricks; pale rose, crimson, blood red, shades of orange and bluish brown. Twisted chimneys. Panelled rooms. Plaster ceilings. Perhaps, the most romantic of all England's country houses. Sadly, no longer open. May be glimpsed through the trees from the nearby road.

Stanway House, Stanway

Bourton House Garden, Bourton-on-the-Hill

ARBORETA & GARDENS

Batsford Arboretum & Wild Garden. 56 acres of rare and beautiful trees are part of one of the largest private collection of trees in Britain. The Japanese Cherries are stunning. Open daily 10-4.40. 01386 701441 www.batsarb.co.uk

Blockley, Mill Dene Garden. A beautiful 2 1/2 acres set aroundan historic water mill. Rose terrace, grotto and trout stream. Lunches and teas. Open Apr-Sept, W-Su from 10, except in July. 01386 700457 www.milldenegarden.co.uk

Bourton House Garden. 3 acres of intense planting; topiary, knot garden, potager and a profusion of herbaceous borders and exotic plants. The wonderful tithe barn is host to a gallery of contemporary arts and crafts. Lunches and teas. Pre-booked groups only. Open Apr-Oct W-F 10-5. 01386 700754 www.bourtonhouse.com

Hidcote Manor Garden (NT). One of the finest gardens of the C20 designed by Major Lawrence Johnston in the Arts & Crafts style. It is made up of garden rooms with rare trees, shrubs, herbaceous borders and 'old' roses. The all-weather court has recently been restored. Barn café, plant sales and restaurant. Open mid-Mar to Oct M Tu W & W/Es, 10-6 (-5 in Oct) & some winter W/Es 01386 438333 www.nationaltrust.org.uk

Kiftsgate Court Garden. Rare shrubs, plants, and an exceptional collection of roses in a magnificent situation. Water Garden. Plants for sale. Open Days. Open Apr & Sept Su, M & W 2-6. May-July Sa-W 12-6, Aug Sa-W 2-6. 01386 438777 www.kiftsgate.co.uk

Little Malvern Court & Gardens. Former Benedictine monastery. Home of the Russell and Berington families since the Dissolution. Priors Hall with needlework, family and European furniture and paintings. 10 acre garden; spring bulbs, rose garden and views. Open mid-Apr to mid-July W & Th only 2.15-5. 01684 892988

Malmesbury, Abbey House Gardens. The home of the Naked Gardeners, so be prepared for a surprise and some excitement amidst the tulips! View their website for Clothes Optional Days. There are bulbs galore, especially the 70,000 tulips in Spring and a massive range of 2,200 different roses, herbaceous borders, specimen trees and shrubs. Open daily 21 Mar to 21 Oct 11-5.30. 01666 822212 www.abbeyhousegardens.co.uk

Hidcote Manor Garden, Chipping Campden

North Cerney, Cerney House Gardens. Just look around and you know it has been created by persons of immense enthusiasm, passion and experimentation. And you have a garden of maturity, too. Old roses and herbaceous borders sit well beside the walled kitchen/flower garden. You may purchase plants from their important plant collections. Open daily Feb-Oct 10-5. 01285 831300 www.cerneygardens.com

Painswick, Rococo Garden. A beautiful C18 Rococo garden in 6 acres dating from a period of flamboyant and romantic garden design nestles in a hidden Cotswold valley. Be sure you visit in February for the display of magical snowdrops. Open daily mid-Jan to Oct, 11-5. Restaurant and Gift Shop. 01452 813204 www.rococogarden.co.uk

Westonbirt Arboretum

Rococo Garden, Painswick

Westonbirt Arboretum. If you believe trees to be the most beautiful things in creation then a visit to this wonderland must be at the top of your agenda. Here, in this arboreal paradise garden, you will find 600 acres of magnificent trees and shrubs from around the world. With no less than 15,500 individual specimens of 3,000 different tree types, and a good 17 miles of footpaths ahead, you will need comfy footwear. Needless to say, it is quite a sight in spring and autumn, and popular too. Oak Hall Visitor Centre, giftshop and courtyard cafe. Plant centre. Open daily 9-dusk, from 8 at W/Es. 01666 880220 www.forestry.gov.uk/westonbirt

You may also like to consider:

Alkerton, Brook Cottage. Four acre Hillside garden surrounding C17 house (closed). Over 200 shrubs and colour co-ordinated borders, climbing roses, clematis, alpine and water gardens. Plant stall/teas. Open East M-Oct M-F 9-6. 01295 670303 www.brookcottagegarden.co.uk

Kemerton, The Priory Garden. Long herbaceous borders in colour groups. Stream and water garden. 4 acres. Redesigned walled garden. Unusual plants for sale. Open every Th July to Sept 2-6, and various Su (Teas). 01386 725258

Misarden Park Gardens. The home of the Wills family, of tobacco fame has shrubs, a traditional rose garden, perennial borders, extensive yew topiary, magnolia Goulangeana and spring bulbs amidst a picturesque woodland setting. Rill and Summerhouse. The Elizabethan mansion has mullion windows and was extended by Waterhouses in the C19 and by Lutyens who added a new wing between 1920-21. The gardens are open Apr to Sept Tu, W & Th, 10-4.30. Nursery open daily except M, Apr to mid-Oct. 01285 821303 www.misardenpark.co.uk

Upper Swell, Abbotswood. Manor house altered by Sir Edwin Lutyens. Extensive heather and stream gardens. Formal terraced gardens. Plantings of spring bulbs. Open for National Gardens Scheme. 01451 830173

Westbury Court Garden (NT). C17 Dutch water garden laid out between 1696 and 1705. Designed with canals, yew hedge and vegetable plots. Open East to Oct W-Su & BH Ms 10-5. Open daily July & Aug 10-5. 01452 760461 www.nationaltrust.org.uk

COUNTRYSIDE INTERESTS

Arlingham, St Augustine's Farm. Working farm where you can explore the 50 organic acres, stroke and feed the animals, and buy free range eggs. Open Mar to Oct Tu-Su 11 5. 01452 740277 www.staugustinesfarm.co.uk

Bibury Trout Farm. This working trout farm lies in a beautiful setting beside the River Coln. You can feed the fish, or try your hand at fly fishing in the Beginner's Fishery (hours vary). There are fresh and prepared trout on sale, as well as plants and shrubs. Gift shop. Light refreshments. Open summer M-Sa 8-6, Su 10-6, winter daily 8-4. 01285 740215 www.biburytroutfarm.co.uk

Bourton-On-The-Water, Adam Henson's Cotswold Farm Park. A unique survival centre for rare historic breeds of British farm animals including the Cotswold Lions (the Golden Fleece), is elevated high on the Central Wolds, three miles from Bourton. Pets and tots corner. Farm trail. Lambing, shearing and seasonal exhibitions. Café. Camp Site. Open daily, all year 10.30-5. 01451 850307 www.cotswoldfarmpark.co.uk

Bourton-On-The-Water, Santhill Fisheries. Mature 26-acre lake stocked with Rainbow and Brown Trout. Day, half-day, evening tickets and boat hire. Open Mar to 21 Dec. 01451 810291 The Lakes. These are flooded gravel pits from the 1960s and 70s. Now used for a carp farm, windsurfing centre and angling lake. There is a great abundance of wildlife: plants, insects and birds.

Cotswold Water Park, South Cerney

Bredons Hardwick, Croft Farm Leisure & Water Park. Lake and river fishing, camping, windsurfing tuition, and supervised health centre. Open daily Mar to Dec. 01684 772321 www.croftfarmleisure.co.uk

Snowshill, Cotswold Lavender. Fields to roam in. Tearoom. Plants. Shop. Open daily 10-5 in summer, W-Su Sept-Dec. 01386 854821 www.cotswold-lavender.co.uk

South Cerney, Cotswold Water Park. This covers an area of 40 square miles of countryside and is split into three sections: the Western section, the Keynes Country Park and the Eastern Section (near Fairford). There are 140 lakes, 74 fishing lakes, 10 lakes with SSSI status, 40 different lake owners and 150km of pathways, bridleways and cycleways. 20,000 people live in the park's 14 main settlements. The extraction of the gravel and sand deposits from

Bibury Trout Farm

Cotswold Lions, Cotswold Farm Park

the 'catchment area' of the Upper Thames left large holes that were in 1967 designated to become a water park. From its humble beginnings at the South Cerney Sailing Club the park now attracts more than half-a-million visitors a year. Children love the sandy beach and sculptures at Keynes whilst the more active are beckoned to the wakeboarding and slalom skis at WM Ski on Spine Road www.wmski.com A visit to the Gateway Centre on Spine Road is recommended before you explore the park where you can eat and drink at the Coot's Café daily from 9-5. Just opposite is the retailer Cotswold Outdoor for all your walking and camping supplies. Further down the road overlooking Spring Lake, the Lakeside Brasserie for coffees, beers, pizzas, burgers and childrens meals www.watermarkclub.co.uk

Lechlade & Bushleaze Trout Fisheries. Stocked with Brown and Rainbow trout (the odd Pike) for day and half-day, and evening fishing. Tackle shop, loos, tuition and boat hire on hand. 01367 253266 www.lechladetrout.co.uk

Northleach, Lloyd Baker Countryside Collection, The Old Prison. Fascinating medley of agricultural implements: carts and bygone machinery. Open Apr-Oct W-Sa 11-4.

Nympsfield, Thistledown Environment Centre. Promotes the awareness of agricultural and environmental practices by tackling ecological issues head on in a fun way. Follow the adventure, sculpture and wildlife trails. Organic campsite. Open daily Apr-Oct 10-5.30, or sundown. 01453 860420 www.thistledown.org.uk

You may also like to consider:

Tewkesbury, John Moore Countryside Museum, 41 Church Street. Dedicated to children and all aspects of nature conservation displayed in a C15 timber framed house. Open Apr to Oct Tu-Sa & BHs, 10-1 & 2-5. 01684 297174

Witney, Cogges Manor Farm Museum, Church Lane. Historic buildings, exhibitions, traditional breeds of animals, daily demos and special weekends. Garden, orchard and riverside walk. Café. Open Apr to Oct Tu-F & BH Ms 11-5, W/Es 12-5.30. Manor House open W/Es & BHs with guided tour F's at 11 am. 01993 772602 www.cogges.org.uk

Cotswold Lavender

Daylesford Organic Farm Shop, Moreton in Marsh

FARM SHOPS

Birdwood, Smart's Tradition Gloucester Cheeses. Family farm where Double and Single Gloucester cheese-making can be watched. Open Tu & Th. Phone for details: 01452 750225.
www.smartsgloucestercheese.com

Broadway, Barnfield Winery & Cider Mill. Famous cider and country wines. Museum. Open daily 10-6, all year. 01386 853145
www.barnfieldcidermill.co.uk

Chedworth Farm Shop. If you seek fresh produce, none better, for here they have a Butchery, Dairy, Fruit & Veg, Ice Cream, fish and chips, and a camp site. Open daily from 9 M-Sa, Su from 10. 01285 720265
www.cotswoldfarmfayre.com

Cirencester, The Organic Farm Shop, Burford Road. A working farm, and eco destination: 'Eating organic is eating from the Earth, Back to nature void of pesticides. All growing freely without insecticides.' Café/restaurant. Camping. Open from 9 Tu-Sa, Su from 11. 01285 640441
www.theorganicfarmshop.co.uk

Daylesford Organic Farm Shop. Its all so pristine clean and perfect one wonders if the clientele have ever seen a truck fill of manure, or been inside a pig shed. The old adage, "Where There's Muck, There's Brass" may be an apt description here if you can find the muck but the prices are high, and the quality of the produce is not in question. For a farm boy it doesn't quite ring true. Kitchen, Bakery & Café. Open daily. 01603 731700
wwwdaylesfordorganic.com

Donnington Fish Farm. Spring-fed; fresh trout, smoked trout and paté. Open Tu-Sa 10-5.30 (-5 in winter). 01451 830873
www.go-fish.co.uk

Frocester Fayre Farm Shop. Purveyors of fine meats; all the pork and beef are reared on the farm, as is the poultry. Open M- F 8-5, Sa 9-12.30. T 01453 822054
www.frocesterfayre.co.uk

Great Rollright, Wyatts Countryside Centre. Farm shop with ice cream parlour in organic conversion plus a garden nursery, animal and play area, and restaurant. Open daily, 9-5.30. 01608 684835

Hayles Fruit Farm. Wide range of locally produced fruit, cider and home-cured hams. Tearoom. Two nature trails. Camping. Open daily. 01242 602123
www.hayles-fruit-farm.co.uk

Shurdington, Primrose Vale Farm Shop & PYO. Fruit and vegetables are grown here, and you can PYO. Organic meats, cheeses and bakeries are supplied from local producers. Open M-Sa from 9, Su from 10. T 01452 863359
www.primrosevale.com

South Cerney, Butts Farm (& Farm Shop). Rare breeds, sheep, fowl, pigs and cattle in 30 acres of meadowland. Tractor safari. Picnics. Pets' corner. Open East-Sept Tu-Su & BHs 10.30-5. (daily in hols & half-term) 01285 862224
www.thebuttsfarmshop.com

BIRDS & WILDLIFE

Batsford Park, Cotswold Falconry Centre. Dedicated to the conservation of eagles, hawks, falcons and owls, with many breeding pairs. Flying displays throughout the day. New parliament of owls. Open daily mid-Feb to mid- Nov, 10.30-5.30. 01386 701043
www.cotswold-falconry.co.uk

Berkeley, Butterfly House. See Berkeley Castle.

Berkeley, Cattle Country Adventure Park. Unusual breeds of cattle, with wild boar in special enclosures. Play area. Pets corner. Open daily Easter-Oct, 10-5.
www.cattlecountry.co.uk

Bourton-On-The-Water, Birdland Park & Gardens. Home to over 500 birds on banks of the River Windrush: Penguins, tropical and sub-tropical birds. Feed the penguins and adopt a bird. Open daily Apr to Oct 10-6, Nov to Mar 10-4. 01451 820480
www.birdland.co.uk

Burford, Cotswold Wildlife Park. A full score of animals, birds and reptiles from all corners of the globe beautifully laid out in 120 acres of gardens and

Cotswold Falcony Centre, Batsford Park, Moreton in Marsh

parkland. Adventure playground. Tropical House. Children's farmyard. Facilities for the disabled. Picnic area. Café. Open daily from 10. 01993 823006
www.cotswoldwildlifepark.co.uk

Elver Fishing. The elver is a baby eel which arrives here in Spring after a two-year journey from the Sargasso Sea. They are fished with nets at Epney on the Severn and considered to be a culinary delicacy (if parboiled and fried in bacon fat), and are reputed to be aphrodisiac in effect. The elvers mature in isolated ponds then return across the Atlantic to spawn. On Easter Monday, Frampton on Severn holds an elver eating contest. The winners are then allowed to rest in a quiet bedchamber.

Evesham Country Park & Vale Wildlife Centre. Wildlife rescue centre supporting animal welfare. Set in country park that has fishing, walks, café and garden centre. Open daily from 10.30. 01386 882288
www.vwr.org.uk

Honeybourne, Domestic Fowl Trust. A collection of rare and minority breeds; hens, turkeys, ducks, geese and farm animals in grass paddocks. New Visitor Centre. Playground. Teas. Camping. Open daily 9.30-5. 01386 833083
www.domesticfowltrust.co.uk

Hook Norton, Waterfowl Sanctuary & Rescue Centre. A centre for rare breeds, with an emphasis on giving children a 'hands-on' experience with the farm animals. Baby barn. Open Tu-Su 10.30-5 (Dusk). 01608 730252
www.waterfowlsanctuary.co.uk

Prinknash Bird Park. Collection of over 50 wildfowl, waterfowl and tame deer. Open daily from 10. 01452 812727
www.prinknash-bird-and-deerpark.com

You may also like to consider:

Gloucestershire Wildlife Trust, Robinswood Hill Country Park. Visitor Centre, exhibition and giftshop. Open daily 9-5, W/Es 11-4.30. 01452 383333
www.gloucestershirewildlifetrust.co.uk

Slimbridge, Wildfowl & Wetlands Trust. Founded by the late Sir Peter Scott in 1946, and home to the world's largest collection of flamingos, swans, geese and ducks - with over 35,000 wildfowl in winter. In historic terms it is most probably the birthplace of modern conservation. Restaurant. Shop. Picnic areas. Free wheelchairs for the disabled. Open daily 9.30-5.30 (-5 in winter). 01453 891900
www.wwt.org.uk

Twigworth, Nature In Art Museum, Wallsworth Hall. The World's first Museum dedicated exclusively to Art inspired by nature. Life-size sculptures in the garden. Artists, in Residence. Coffee Shop. Open Tu-Su & BHs 10-5. 01452 731422
www.nature-in-art.org.uk

Flamingos, Wildfowl & Wetlands Trust, Slimbridge

Broadway Tower Walk, Broadway

COUNTRY PARKS, THE NATURAL WORLD & RIVER VALLEYS

Bourton Lakes. These are flooded gravel pits from the 1960s and 70s. Now used for a carp farm, windsurfing centre and angling lake. There is a great abundance of wildlife: plants, insects and birds.

Broadway Tower Country Park. A unique Cotswold attraction: an C18 folly tower with historical and geographical exhibitions. Country retreat of the pre-Raphaelite, William Morris. Breeders of red deer with adventure playground, nature walks, barbecue and restaurant. Superb views from the top of the Tower – a clear day gives a view of 12 counties. Open Apr to Oct 10.30-5, Nov to Mar W/Es 11-3. 01386 852390 www.broadwaytower.co.uk

Churn Valley. A memorable route from Seven Springs to Cirencester follows one of England's most scenic drives. The variety of the trees and the sunken river valley are a sight to behold. Beware, this is a fast road and accidents are frequent.

Cirencester Park. Belongs to the Bathurst family who have generously opened their grounds for many years giving you the opportunity to walk in 3,000 acres of landscaped parkland, and along a five-mile avenue of horse chestnuts and hardwoods that were planted in the early C18. The C18 mansion is home to Lord Apsley and is not open to the general public. If you like hobnobbing with celebrities you have the opportunity to do so by watching polo on most Sundays at 3pm, from May to September, see: www.cirencesterpolo.co.uk or 01285 640410. The park opens daily all year from 8-5. Separate entrance to the Cricket and Tennis clubs on the Stroud road. www.cirencesterpark.co.uk

Devil's Chimney, Leckhampton, Cheltenham

Croome Park (NT), Nr Pershore. 'Capability' Brown's first significant landscape project. A restoration plan has begun - dredging and replanting the Lake Garden. Open Mar,Sept & Oct W-Su, daily Apr to Aug, Xmas & Jan W/Es, 11-5. 01905 371006 www.nationaltrust.org.uk

Devil's Chimney, Leckhampton. A 50 foot high limestone rock which according to local superstition 'rises from hell.' Its origins resulted from quarrying the surrounding stone.

Coln Valley. Charming valley with typically quaint Cotswold villages: Ablington, Calcot, Coln Rogers, Coln St Dennis, and Winson.

Golden Valley. Runs from Sapperton to Chalford, and is especially fine with the arrival of the Autumnal colours of beech, ash and oak.

Highnam Woods Nature Reserve. 300 acres of broad-leafed woodland, with bluebells in spring. Nightingales call (if you are listening). Open daily. 01594 562852 www.rspb.org.uk

Leckhampton Hill. A popular dog walking area for Cheltonians providing superb views towards the Malvern Hills and Wales. The golden stone of 'Regency' Cheltenham was quarried here. Iron Age and Roman camps.

You may also like to consider:

Macaroni Downs, Eastleach. Quite a sight. These rolling sheep pastures were once the location for Regency derring-do, gambling and horse racing. Now just munched by sheep.

Seven Springs, Coberley. One of the Sources of the River Thames. There is a stone plaque here with a Latin inscription which reads, roughly translated: 'Here thou, O Father Thames, hast thy sevenfold beginning'.

River Coln, Calcot

Sherborne Park Estate (NT). Waymarked walks through woods and parkland with fine views. www.nationaltrust.org.uk

The Bottoms; Waterley Bottom, Tyley Bottom and Ozleworth Bottom. Deep combes (valleys) of rare and solitary beauty rich in wild flowers and bird life. And all can be viewed from countless footpaths. Strange to believe, but in the C17 and C18 Waterley operated 15 fulling mills (to cleanse and thicken cloth) within a radius of 5 miles.

Windrush Valley. A slow, trickling stream in summer with a tendency to flood in winter. The river snakes its way through quiet golden villages, creating the idyllic Cotswold scene.

Sherborne Brook

Bull in Field, Coln Valley

Cam Long Down

WOODLAND & OPEN SPACE WALKS

Chalford Valley Nature Trail. Passes beside the River Frome and the Thames & Severn Canal. Parking near Round House by the Industrial Estate.

Chedworth Woods. A network of footpaths that criss-cross through tangled woodland close to the Roman Villa.

Coombe Hill Canal Nature Reserve. Two-mile stretch of canal closed in 1876. Habitat of birds, dragonflies, aquatic and bankside plants. Open all year.

Cooper's Hill, Nr Brockworth. 137 acres of common land in which to roam wild,criss-crossed by nature trails. Start from the car park at Fiddler's Elbow. The scene of the Cheese-Rolling ceremony on Whit Monday at 6pm – a large cheese (originally representing the Sun in a Pagan ceremony) is chased down the hill. Only for the fittest, and craziest at heart, for limbs have known to be fractured here on many occasions. Scene of an Iron Age fort.

Cranham Woods. Bluebells and white garlic bloom in Spring, and a web of footpaths are spread throughout this tangled woodland.Best approached from Birdlip in early summer when the foliage is green and new.

Ebworth Estate (NT), Sheepscombe. Woodland walks through beech woods Rich in wildlife managed by English Nature. No parking facilities.01452 814213

Fish Hill Woods, Broadway Hill. Attractive woodland providing superb views.

Bluebells

Minchinhampton Common (NT). A wide, open space popular with dog walkers, horse riding, golfers and the ancient Saxons final resting place - see the Long Barrows and Earthworks.

Rodborough Common (NT). 800 acres of open space provides great walks and views across the Stroud Valleys.

Wychwood Forest, Charlbury. Formerly a Royal Hunting forest. The around Cornbury Park is richly wooded and makes for a fine 9-mile circular walk. Start beside the Bull in Charlbury.

THE COTSWOLD WAY

A long distance footpath covering 97 miles, from Chipping Campden to Bath. It follows the edge of the escarpment, meanders through picturesque villages, past pre-historic sites, and provides spectacular views. It is waymarked. For short excursions set out from the following:-
www.cotswold-way.co.uk

Brackenbury Ditches., North Nibley. This is an impregnable Iron Age fort, and a splendid viewpoint with views across the Severn Vale, and Welsh Mountains.

Broadway Tower. Starting from the Tower you can make a circular walk of 2.5 miles to Broadway and back.

Cam Long Down Nr Cam. A humpbacked ridge of oolitic limestone that once seen is never forgotten. From the top it's a good viewpoint surrounded by beech woods and bracken.

Cleeve Hill. At 1,083 feet this is the highest point in the Cotswolds and thus a superb viewpoint across to the Malvern Hills, Welsh Mountains, and northwards across the Cotswold landscape. A popular dog walking area and, in winter snow, ideal for tobaggan runs. In 1901 a tramway was built from Cheltenham to Cleeve Cloud but sadly closed in 1930. Cleeve Cloud is the site of an Iron Age hill fort and just below the scarp is The Ring, a site of religious/pagan rituals, 100 feet in diameter. Castle Rock is popular with novice rock climbers.

Cleeve Common. A vast expanse of common land where you are free to roam, with dog and friends. It is more like a piece of wild moorland with its extensive horizons, and you may be forgiven for believing you are in the midst of a National Park. There are wild flowers, the Gallops (for exercising race horses) and tracks that lead off in all directions. Park in the golf course, or in the lay-byes, on the B4632.

Crickley Hill Country Park. Nature trails, geological and archaeological trails are signposted, as is the Cotswold Way. There are traces of Stone Age and Iron Age settlements. Fine views. Open daily.

Coaley Peak. On the edge of the Cotswold escarpment affording fine views. Picnic area. Ice Cream van.

Dover's Hill. A natural amphitheatre on a spur of the Cotswolds with magnificent views over the Vale of Evesham. The 'Olympick Games & Scuttlebrook Wake' have been held here since 1612, and take place the Friday and Saturday following the Spring Bank Holiday.

Frocester Hill. A superb viewpoint rising to 778 feet provides superb views over the Severn Estuary, Welsh Hills and Forest of Dean.

Haresfield Beacon & Standish Wood (NT). High open grassland at 700 feet that was a natural fort held by Iron Age and Roman settlements. Delightful when the bluebells and primroses bloom in the Spring.

View from Coaley Peak, Cotswold Way

TRANSPORT INTERESTS

Banbury, Oxford Canal. Built by James Brindley in 1769 to connect the industrial Midlands with London via the River Thames. Financial problems delayed the construction but it was eventually to reach Oxford in 1789. Today, it runs for 77 miles from Hawkesbury Junction, south of Coventry to Oxford. You can enjoy a multitude of leisure activities, from solitary walks to boating, canoeing, cycling, fishing and the wildlife.
www.waterscape.com

Banbury, Tooley's Boatyard & Tours, Spiceball Park Road. This is the oldest working dry dock boatyard on the inland waterways of Britain. Established in 1790 to build and repair the wooden horse-drawn narrow boats. 200-year old forge, chandlery and gift shop. Self drive hire and private boat trips. 01295 272917 www.tooleysboatyard.co.uk

Bourton-On-The-Water, Cotswold Motoring Museum. Motorcycles and vintage racing cars in an C18 water mill. Collection of old advertising signs. Open daily mid-Feb to mid-Dec 10-6. 01451 821255 www.cotswold-motor-museum.com

Bourton-On-The-Water, Model Railway. Over 500 sq.ft. of exhibits. Continental trains and British Railway trains in HO/OO and N Gauge. Open daily June-Aug, Sept-May W/Es, 11-5. 01451 820686 www.bourtonmodelrailway.co.uk

Cotswold Canals. The Stroudwater Navigation was opened in 1779 linking Stroud to the River Severn in order to serve the cloth industry of the Stroud Valleys. The Thames and Severn Canal was built to link the Stroudwater to the River Thames via the Sapperton Tunnel. The towpath is open and the best places to see the restored canal are at Eastington, near Stonehouse and at both portals of the Sapperton Tunnel, and west of the Spine Road in the Cotswold Water Park. The restoration work is on-going and is actively creating freshwater habitats where wildflowers abound, notably 'Lilies of the Valley'.01285 643440 www.cotswoldcanals.com

Gloucester & Sharpness Canal. Opened in 1827 and built above the River Severn. It's 16 miles long and was originally used by ocean-going ships in transit to Gloucester.

Gloucester Waterways Museum, Llanthony Warehouse. A major national exhibition about the history of the inland waterways. Historic boats and leisure cruises on hand: 01452 318200. Café. Open daily 11-4 (July-Aug 10.30-5) 01452 318200 www.nwm.org.uk

Oxford Bus Museum, BR Station Goods Yard. 35 vehicles including the Morris Motors Museum. Open Su, W & BHs 10.30-4.30. (& summer Sa) 01993 883617 www.oxfordbusmuseum.org.uk

Oxford Canal, Banbury

Tall Ships, Gloucester Docks

Thames and Severn Canal, Coates

Prescott Hill, Bugatti Trust. A small exhibition illustrates the work of Ettore Bugatti the genius of industrial design and invention. Study Centre with drawings, photos and some cars. Open M-F 10-4, and during Hill Climb days. 01242 677201 www.bugatti-trust.co.uk

Toddington, North Gloucestershire Railway. Steam hauled narrow - gauge Railway and museum. Trains operate From East to Oct Su & BHs 12-5. www.toddington-narrow-gauge.co.uk

You may also like to consider:

Winchcombe, Railway Museum, 23 Gloucester Street. Relics and bygones including operating exhibits in a peaceful Cotswold garden. Open daily East to Oct 1.30-6. Winter W/Es & BHs 1.30-dusk. 01242 609305 www.winchcomberailwmusem.co.uk

SS Jaguar, Cotswold Motoring Museum

Cotswold Woollen Weavers, Filkins

INDUSTRIAL INTERESTS

Beckford Silk. Hand printers of silk. Gallery of textiles. Factory tours. Coffee shop 10-4. Open M-Sa 10-5. 01386 881507
www.beckfordsilk.co.uk

Chipping Campden, Harts Silversmiths - The Old Silk Mill. Founded in 1888 as part of the 'Arts & Crafts' movement. The Harts gold and silversmith workshop is the last operating remnant of the Guild of Handicraft which C R Ashbee established in 1888, and which moved to this village in 1902. Café. Open all year. 01386 841100
www.hartsilversmiths.co.uk

Donnington Brewery. Established in 1865 by Thomas Arkell who used the spring water to concoct his delicious potions. The brewery remains independent and supplies 15 tied houses and a number of free trade outlets.
www.donnington-brewery.com

Filkins, Cotswold Woollen Weavers. A visit here is a "Must" for all who wish to learn about the Cotswolds; the story of wool and woollen cloth has woven its way into every fabric of Cotswold life, as has the stone that built the barns, churches and villages. The stone is displayed by the masons' sculptures and workmanship. The cloth, and the garments made up in their many guises (scarves, throws, jackets, as well as rolls of cloth) mirror the eccentricities of this unique establishment. Large mill shop & interiors gallery. Coffee shop. Picnic area. Masonry yard. Open daily M-Sa 10-6, Su 2-6. 01367 860491
www.cotswoldwollenweavers.co.uk

Hook Norton Brewery. Visitor Centre displays brewing artifacts from 1849 to today. Open all year M-Sa & BHs, 9.30-4.30. Two-hour tours from 11. 01608 737210
www.hooky.co.uk

Stroud Mills: Dunkirk Mill Centre. A mill with machinery driven by the largest working water wheel in Gloucestershire. Displays on the finishing processes of fulling, teasel raising and cross cutting. Access is via the Cycle Track by Egypt Mill. Open Apr to Sept on odd W/Es 2-4. 01453 766273
www.stroud-textile.org.uk

Gigg Mill, Old Bristol Road. Historic mill with weaving shed containing ancient and modern looms. Open as Dunkirk Mill, above. Ruskin Mill. A thriving arts, craft and education centre set in a restored 1820s woollen mill. 01453 837521
www.rmet.co.uk

St Mary's Mill, Chalford. An 1820 mill housing a large water wheel and a powerful Tangye steam engine. Open for Open Days on 01453 766273

Stanley Mill, Stonehouse. Built in 1812, the mill has an exceptional interior where you can watch demonstrations of wool carding and mule spinning. To visit book on 01453 766273

Uley, The Old Brewery. The mill owner, Samuel Price built this brewery in 1833 to assuage his workers thirst. It was restored in 1984 and has since won many awards for their Old Spot, Pigs Ear and Uley Bitter. It is not open to prying visitors, only the trade. You can sample their wares in the Old Crown Inn at the top of the village, or in various hostelries around the Cotswolds.

Gallery Pangolin, Chalford ss

WORKING CRAFTMANSHIP

Bourton-On-The-Water, Cotswold Pottery. Traditional rustic pots, hand-thrown using local materials. Bronze sculptures too. Open M-Sa 10-4, Su 11-4. 01451 820173
www.cotswoldpottery.co.uk

Chalford, Gallery Pangolin. Specializes in modern and contemporary bronze sculptures that have been caste in their foundry, and also sculptures' drawings. Open M-F 10-6, Sa 10-1. 01453 886527
www.gallery-pangolin.com

Conderton Pottery. Distinctive stoneware pots by specialist salt glazed country potter, Toff Milway. Open M-Sa 9-5. 01386 725387.
www.toffmilway.co.uk

Hook Norton, Hamish Mackie Wildlife Sculptor, Manor Farm Barn. Hamish grew up on a livestock farm in Cornwall and his sculptures have benefited from this early exposure to English wildlife. 01608 737859
www.hamishmackie.com

Hook Norton Pottery & Craft Centre. Workshop and gallery open all year. Local crafts including paintings, basketware, woodcraft and cards. Open M-Sa 9-5.01608 737414
www.hooknortonpottery.co.uk

Painswick Woodcrafts, 3 New St. Dennis French specializes in British woodware, hand-turned on the lathe - table lamps, bowls, vases. Open F-Sa & BH Ms 10-4. 01452 814195
www.painswickwoodcrafts.co.uk

Stroud, Lansdown Pottery. A small group of potters work here developing their own different styles. It is also a centre or learning and art shows with the Studio, Glaze room, Kiln Room and extensive Library. Open M-F 10-5. 01453 753051
www.lansdownpottery.co.uk

Whichford Pottery. Hand-made English terracotta flowerpots of immense size. Thirty craftsmen and women. Shop. Open daily M-F 9-5, Sa 10-4. 01608 684416
www.whichfordpottery.com

Winchcombe Pottery. One of the country's most respected potteries, known throughout the ceramic world. A large variety of hand-made domestic ware on sale in the shop. Open daily M-F 8-5, Sa 10-4 (& Su Apr-Dec 11-4). 01242 602462
www.winchcombepottery.co.uk

Woodstock, Julia Beusch Gallery, 25 Oxford Street. Gallery of modern jewellery. Original and exquisite designs. Open Tu-F 10-6, Sa 10-5. 01993 813445
www.juliabeusch.co.uk

Mike Finch, Winchcombe Pottery

Keith Harding's World of Mechanical Music, Northleach

MUSEUMS

Berkeley, Edward Jenner Museum. A Queen Anne House with traditional and modern displays that celebrate the life of Edward Jenner, the surgeon who discovered a vaccine for smallpox. Open Apr to Sept, Tu-Sa 12.30-5.30, Su & BH Ms 1-5.30, & daily June to Aug, Oct Su 1-5.30. 01453 810631
www.jennermuseum.com

Broadway, Gordon Russell Museum, 15 Russell Square. A collection spanning 60 years that is dedicated to one of the C20s finest furniture designers. With original design drawings and furniture embracing the 'Arts & Crafts' movement. Open Tu-Su 11-4 & BH Ms. 01386 854695
www.gordonrussellmuseum.org

Cheltenham, Art Gallery & Museum, Clarence Street. Re-opening in October after a major restoration with a world-renowned Arts & Crafts Movement collection inspired by William Morris. Rare Chinese, and English ceramics. Social history of Cheltenham. C17 Dutch and C17-20 British paintings. Host to the Gloucestershire Guild of Craftsmen. Open daily 10-5 (-4 Nov-Mar). Closed BHs. 01242 237431
www.cheltenhammuseum.org.uk

Cheltenham, Gustav Holst Birthplace Museum, Clarence Road. Pittville. Memorabilia of the composer's life. Period Furnished rooms. Open all year Tu-Sa 10-4, Su 1.30-5. Closed mid-Dec to Feb. 01242 524846
www.holstmuseum.org.uk

Chipping Campden, Court Barn Museum. A celebration of the town's association with the "Arts & Crafts Movement". An exhibition of silver, jewellery ceramics, sculpture, industrial design and more, all beautifully set up by the Guild of Handicraft Trust. Open Tu-Sa 10-5 & BH Ms (-4 Oct to Mar)
www.courtbarn.org.uk

Cirencester, Corinium Museum. Impressive collection of Roman remains clearly displayed to relate the development of the Cotswolds from the earliest times with special reference to the Roman period. Open daily all year M-Sa 10-5, Su 2-5. Attached to Jack's Coffee Shop. 01285 655611
www.coriniummuseum.co.uk

Gloucester, City Museum & Art Gallery, Brunswick Road. Recently undergone a major restoration project; Roman relics, dinosaurs, aquarium, art exhibitions. Open Tu-Sa 10-5. (D9) 01452 396131
www.gloucester.gov.uk/citymuseum

Gloucester, Folk Museum, 99-103 Westgate Street. Medieval timber-framed buildings associated with martyrdom of Bishop Hooper in 1555. Social history, folklore, crafts and industries of city and county. Herb garden. Open Tu-Sa 10-5. 01452 396868 www.gloucester.gov.uk/folkmuseum

Lower Slaughter, Old Mill Museum. This iconic C19 flourmill has been lovingly restored into a small museum with ice cream parlour, tea room and mill shop, all overlooking the Mill Leat (pond). The proprietor is the lead singer in a Jazz band, hence the funky music. Open daily (W/Es Jan to Feb), 10-6. 01451 820052 www.oldmill-lowerslaughter.com

Northleach, Keith Harding's World of Mechanical Music. One of the finest attractions in the Cotswolds where you will always be met with a cheery welcome. An enchanting wonderland of mechanical musical instruments, clocks and restored musical boxes. 'Magical Musicals'. Gift shop. Open daily 10-5. 01451 860181 www.mechanicalmusic.co.uk

Stow, Cotswold Cricket Museum, Brewery Yard. A dazzling collection of world artifacts showcase the history of this great game. Coffee shop. Open Tu-Sa 9.30-5, Su 10-4. www.cotswoldcricketmuseum.co.uk

Stroud, Museum In The Park, Stratford Park. Innovative and colourful displays and changing exhibitions ranging from Dinosaurs to the Uley Roman Temple to the world's first lawnmower and contemporary sculpture. Open Apr to Sept Tu-F 10-5, W/Es & BHs 11-5. Oct to Mar Tu-F 10-4, W/Es 11-4. 01453 763394 www.museuminthepark.org.uk

Woodstock, Oxfordshire Museum, Park Street. An impressive and coherent exhibition of Oxfordshire, and its people, from earliest times to the present day. Changing exhibitions. Coffee shop. Open daily Tu-Sa 10-5, Su 2-5. 01993 811456 www.oxfordshire.gov.uk

Old Mill Museum, Lower Slaughter

John Davies Gallery ss

CONTEMPORARY ART

Burford, Brian Sinfield Gallery, 27 The Hill.
Highly respected gallery featuring changing exhibitions of modern and contemporary paintings, sculpture and ceramics. Open Tu-Sa, 10-5. 01993 824464
www.briansinfield.com

Burford, Salt Gallery, 34 Lower High St. The work of some of Britain's most respected potters and glassmakers; Norman Stuart Clarke, Will Shakspeare, Steve Harrison… Open daily 10-5. 01993 822371
www.saltgallery.com

Cheltenham, Martin's Gallery, Montpellier Parade. Bright gallery with an interest in Asian art. Open W-Sa 11-6. 01242 526044
www.martinsgallery.co.uk

Chipping Campden, Campden Gallery, High Street. One of the most respected of Cotswold galleries has constant changing exhibitions of paintings, sculpture and prints. Open daily Tu-Sa 10-5,30, Su 11-4. 01386 841555
www.campdengallery.co.uk

Cirencester, New Brewery Arts,Brewery Court. A centre for excellence in contemporary arts and crafts with Exhibition Gallery, coffee house, crafts shop, theatre andresident craft workers. Open M-Sa 9-5, Su 10-4. 01285 657181
www.newbreweryarts.org.uk

Campden Gallery

Cirencester, Wet Paint Gallery, 14 London Rd. Colourful, abstract and modern landscapes, ceramics and glass. Open Tu-Sa 10-5. 01285 644990
www.contemporary-art-holdings.co.uk

Fairford, Kim Sutton Gallery, 10 High Street. An exhibition of Dance and Ballerinas - bright watercolour scenes, charcoal drawings and prints. Open M-Sa 10-5, or by appointment. 01285 712500
www.jakesutton.co.uk

Moreton-In-Marsh, John Davies Gallery, The Old Dairy Plant. A much respected Cotswold gallery established in 1977. Six fully catalogued annual exhibitions. Fine period, post Impressionist and contemporary paintings. Open M-Sa 9.30-5. 01608 652255 www.johndaviesgallery.com

Stow, Fosse Gallery, The Square. Well-established gallery displaying paintings; contemporary and modern, most artists are RA, RAI, ROI members. Open Tu-Sa 10.30-5. 01451 831319 www.fossegallery.com

Stow, Red Rag Gallery, Church Street. Original paintings from living artists. Sculpture. Scottish art. Open M-Sa 10-5, Su 10-4. 01451 832563 www.redraggallery.co.uk

And, You May Like To Consider:

Uley, Prema. Independent rural arts centre shows new work by emerging artists in their converted chapel. Open M-F. 01453 860703 www.prema.demon.co.uk

Kim Sutton Gallery, Fairford ss

Wet Paint Gallery ss

New Brewery Arts, Cirencester ss

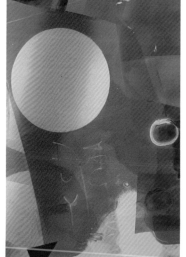

COUNTRY HOUSE & SPA HOTELS

Barnsley House. The former home of the garden expert, the late Rosemary Verey. A chic hotel and spa offering discreet and impeccable service especially recommended for couples released from domestic duties, and great food and state-of-the-art technology. A visit to this extraordinary garden may cost you lunch, but it will be a worthwhile, and memorable experience. Make sure you visit the vegetable garden. Cinema Club. 01285 740000
www.barnsleyhouse.com

Bath, The Royal Crescent Hotel, 16 Royal Crescent. The Royal Crescent occupies two listed buildings which were built by John Wood the Younger and have remained fairly unchanged since the C18. This makes a perfect setting for what is an extravagantly luxurious hotel full of period details. Step into the Royal and you enter a more sumptuous world - one of overstated luxury. Rooms are filled with period details and paintings from C18 masters. Behind the hotel lies a surprise – the beautiful and secluded gardens, perfect for afternoon tea, and overlooked by the Dower House restaurant and bar. The former coach houses are now the Bath House Spa. 01225 823333
www.royalcrescent.co.uk

The Royal Crescent Hotel, Bath

Buckland Manor Hotel, Nr Broadway. The benchmark for the Country House Hotel: quiet, understated luxury, to relax and sooth your investment worries. Formal dress code for dinner for their cuisine demands your sartorial elegance Open all year. 01386 852626
www.bucklandmanor.co.uk

Buckland Manor Hotel

Burford, Bay Tree Hotel, Sheep Street. This is Burford's most luxurious and smartest hostelry, for that is what they are on this old coaching route, hostelries. It is a traditional and charming inn with oak paneled rooms, stone fireplaces and tapestries. Dinner is quite a formal affair. There is a secluded walled garden for pre-prandials and intimate conversation. 01993 822791
www.cotswold-inns-hotels.co.uk/baytree

Calcot Manor, Tetbury. This is a Leisure complex combining an English country hotel furnished in contemporary, up-to-the-minute designs that flow with ease into the C14 Cistercian barns, and all ideally suited for a family, business or leisurely stay. Adjacent you have Calcot Spa for health, beauty and relaxation, and pampering, the Self. And if, after all this hedonism, you need some simple refreshment, a glass of ale, or some nourishment, then pop in to the Gumstool Inn next door. Location is ideal for exploring the southern Cotswolds and Bath. 01666 890391
www.calcotmanor.co.uk

Calcot Manor, Tetbury

Lower Slaughter Manor

Cheltenham, The Greenway, Shurdington. Elizabethan manor house provides elegance, peace and self-indulgent comfort with easy access to the M5 motorway. 01242 862352 www.thegreenway.co.uk

Lower Slaughter Manor. Perfectly proportioned C17 Cotswold manor. Large, spacious rooms furnished with antiques. No children U-12. No dogs. 01451 820456 www.lowerslaughter.co.uk

Painswick, Cotswolds88Hotel, Kemps Lane. This Palladian-style Cotswold rectory has been transformed by interior designer, Marchella De Angelis, into a lifestyle-boutique hotel in homage to the avant-garde artist, Leigh Bowery. Its wacky, bright, eclectic, interesting... it invites opinion. The transformation has been a cause of some controversy, not least from its former owner. One of those places you will either love or hate. Best give it a go. 01452 813688 www.cotswolds88hotel.com

Upper Slaughter, Lords of the Manor. Classy, well-established Country House Hotel, and a firm favourite of US visitors has C17 origins, and is set in eight acres of parkland. Afternoon teas. Child friendly. No dogs. The former home of the Reverend F E B Witts, Rector of this parish who wrote his famous chronicle of the C18, The Diary of a Cotswold Parson. 01451 820243 www.lordsofthemanor.com

Whatley Manor, Easton Grey. Set in a 12-acre traditional English country garden, Whatley Manor is a beautifully restored Cotswold manor house made to feel more like a private home than a hotel. Bedrooms and suites are filled with contemporary and antique furnishings feeding the senses. For those mixing business with pleasure, there is a boardroom and business centre including 40-seat cinema. Spa. 01666 822888 www.whatleymanor.com

Seymour House, Chipping Campden

LUXURY BED & BREAKFAST

Broadway, Mill Hay House. This impressive Queen Anne house provides luxurious B&B on the outskirts of Broadway. No children U-12. No dogs. 01386 852498
www.millhay.co.uk

Cheltenham, Thirty Two, Imperial Square. This is luxury, boutique-style B&B, par excellence. Your hosts are interior designers of exuberance. Just live the dream for a night, or two, and treat yourself. 01242 771110
www.thirtytwoltd.com

Chipping Campden, Seymour House, High Street. Large family home, and one of the villages iconic buildings, all furnished for your every comfort. 01386 840064
www.seymourhousebandb.co.uk

The Library, Lords of the Manor

Cirencester, No.12 Park Street. If style and gracious comfort is to your liking then this Grade II Georgian townhouse offering luxurious B&B may be just what you are looking for. 01285 640232
www.no12cirencester.co.uk

Clapton Manor, Clapton-on-the-Hill. Stunning Grade II listed Tudor house with a beautiful garden created by your host - a garden designer, and historian. 01451 810202
www.claptonmanor.co.uk

Coln St Aldwyns, The Piggery. Sumptuously luxurious and blissful comfort describes this over the top panoply of interior design. Exuberant, exquisite taste. Good value, too. 01285 750719

No 12 Park St, Cirencester

Frampton-On-Severn, The True Heart, The Street. This is a truly sweet little cottage with all the right credentials. It's eco-friendly, fair trade, organic, stylish and comfortable. Within walking distance of the two inns, and a maze of footpaths. 01452 740504
www.thetrueheart.co.uk

Guiting Power, Belstone, Tally Ho! This charming Cotswold cottage is ideally placed to explore the North and Central Wolds walking, cycling and art festivals. 01451 850142

Halford, Old Manor House. English country house style B&B at its finest. From lounging black Labradors to chintz and marmalade, and family antiques. Anyone for tennis? 01789 740264
www.oldmanor-halford.co.uk

Tetbury, Lodge Farm. The owners stock pure bred Hebridean black sheep as well as, thoroughbred horses they are breeding to produce Event horses. Opposite the Elizabethan Mansion Chavenage House. 01666 505339
www.lodgefarm.co.uk

Turkdean, Blanche House. Almost 500 acres of farmland, meadows, woods and ponds surround this picturesque house. Guests are encouraged to explore on foot or horseback. Breakfast in the glass barn overlooking it all. 01451 861176
www.blanchehousebandb.co.uk

Winchcombe, Westward B&B. Sudeley Lodge was built in 1730 as the hunting lodge of Sudeley Castle and guests have included many notable persons such as George III in 1788. The house sits in 550 acres including a beautiful garden with small orchid house and ornamental pond and 80 acres of woodland and a lake. Three en-suite bedrooms. 01242 604372
www.westward-sudeley.co.uk

RESTAURANT WITH ROOMS

Arlingham, The Old Passage. This Restaurant with rooms has a magical and spellbinding quality and the new owners have redecorated the restaurant itself into a light and airy space given to fine views across the Severn, only bettered by the view from the bedrooms above. This continues to be a sea-foodies delight: prawns, devilled whitebait, freshly shucked oyster, Pembrokeshire lobster, roast halibut, the list goes on. Meat, too. Accommodation. Special Severn Bore breakfasts. Closed Ms. 01452 740547
www.theoldpassage.com

Broadway, Russell's, 20 High Street. Now with quite a reputation to hold onto in the North Cotswolds. Feast on their food, then settle into one of their contemporary, comfy bedrooms with all the latest mod cons. Wifi etc.   01386 853555
www.russellsofbroadway.co.uk

The Bell at Sapperton

Chipping Campden, Cotswold House Hotel, The Square. Bespoke luxury, blissful comfort and informality on hand for your every need. Two restaurants; Juliana's (formal) and Hicks' Brasserie, innovative and deliciously sublime. Two bars.01386 840330
www.cotswoldhouse.com

Chipping Campden, Kings Arms, The Square. Handsome Cotswold hotel and brasserie with spacious interior. Drop in for their delicious breakfast, as I did pre-walk. Chic bedroom. French-ambience, to decor. B&B. 01386 840256
www.kingscampden.co.uk

Crudwell, The Rectory. This is a really lovely C16 house that has been transformed into a small, comfortable country house hotel with 12 bedrooms. Three acres with Victorian walled garden, croquet lawn and heated outdoor swimming pool. Beauty and Health therapies on hand. Noted, however, for its superb cuisine. 01666 577194
www.therectoryhotel.com

Kingham, The Plough. The quintessential, loved-by-celebs Cotswold Inn. Yummy food served from the restaurant with a short crawl upstairs to 7 boutique en-suite bedrooms. 01608 658327
www.thekinghamplough.co.uk

Mickleton, Three Ways Hotel (Pudding Club). Home of the Pudding Club, since 1985. Walking tours arranged (to burn off the calories!). Special themed 'Pudding Club' bedrooms. 01386 438429
www.puddingclub.com

Painswick, St Michaels Restaurant. Victoria Street. A family run restaurant with weekly-changing menu. Everything is sourced locally, even berries and wild mushrooms from the nearby fields and hedgerows. Three stylish bedrooms for B&B. 01452 814555
www.stmickshouse.com

Winchcombe, Wesley House, High Street. Deserved reputation for excellent food. Locals travel miles to this gastronomic oasis, and no wonder. Now, with a chic, new wine bar for the local lovelies. Five bedrooms. 01242 602366
www.wesleyhouse.co.uk

Winchcombe, White Hart, High Street. Variously viewed as a pub or a hotel, the White Hart offers quality in both departments. This C16 inn has eight en-suite bedrooms and a bar, restaurant and wine shop. 01242 602359
www.wineandsausage.co.uk

Wesley House, Winchcombe ss

The Wheatsheaf, Northleach ss

DINING PUBS

Alderminster, The Bell. This former C18 coaching inn is now run by the Alscot Estate and has gathered numerous foodie awards. It is spacious, comfortable, and serves good, solid food. Perhaps, more restaurant, than hostelry. 01789 450414
www.thebellald.co.uk

Barnsley, Village Pub. A warren of little rooms serving ambitious pub food and local beers. Child/dog friendly. B&B. Part of the Barnsley House empire, opposite. Beware celebs in mufty. 01285 740421
www.thevillagepub.co.uk

Bledington, The Kings Head Inn. A former C16 cider house, the Kings Head has a dreamlike setting on a village green by a meandering brook. 12 elegant en-suite bedrooms. There's substance under the beauty too with imaginative menus composed of locally produced and organic food. Sister pub to the Swan Inn Swinbrook 01608 658365
www.thekingsheadinn.net

Bourton-on-the-Hill, Horse & Groom. A modern and airy feel permeates this Grade II listed Georgian inn which is peacefully set in a large garden on the hilltop. Bar, en-suite bedrooms and a blackboard menu that changes daily allowing great variety even for the most frequent visitors. 01386 700413
www.horseandgroom.info

Ebrington Arms, Ebrington. An C17 traditional inn full of charm and character and popular with both locals and visitors to the area. Luxurious en-suite bedrooms. Home cooked English breakfast. Closed M except BH Ms. 01386 593223
www.theebringtonarms.co.uk

Northleach, The Wheatsheaf, West End. The success story of Northleach is a friendly C17 coaching inn that invites long hours beside the log fires, and lazy mornings lounging in their comfy beds. Lunch and suppers to be recommended. B&B. Book club. Music nights. 01451 860244 If in Cheltenham try their sister pub, The Tavern, Royal Well Place.
www.cotswoldswheatsheaf.com

Village Pub

Lower Oddington, Fox Inn. One of only 16 Pubs in the country to be Michelin Red Rated, the stone building is hidden behind a sea of Virginia creeper. A reputation for good food, wine and beer and a selection of awards under its belt. B&B. 01451 870555
www.foxinn.net

Paxford, Churchill Arms. Popular and busy local provides sophisticated fayre. Local beers. One of the earliest examples of a gastro-pub. Child friendly. B&B. 01386 594000
www.thechurchillarms.com

Sapperton, The Bell. Popular dining pub given to natural stonewalls, polished flagstone floors, winter log fires provide a comfortable ambience. Local beers. Read the AA Gill Review, hilarious. 01285 760298
www.foodatthebell.co.uk

Stow, The Bell. A recently refurbished inn winning all manner of awards with their food, good sense and hospitality. Music evenings. 5 deluxe bedrooms. 01451 870916
www.thebellatstow.com

The Plough Inn, Ford

TRADITIONAL HOSTELRIES

Asthall, The Maytime Inn. An Authentic Cotswold stone building situated in a quiet country village. On a winter's day you can duck through the low door into the homely bar and imagine the pub as it was centuries ago.   01993 822068
www.themaytime.com

Burford, Lamb Inn, Sheep St. Your typical olde English hostelry: Flagstone floors, low ceilings, nooks and crannies galore, fine ales (Hookie) and now with luxurious bedrooms and intimate lounges. Restaurant. Life can't get any better than this. Yet more informal than its sister inn, The Bay Tree, just along the street.   01993 823155
www.cotswold-inns-hotels.co.uk/lamb

Chedworth, Seven Tuns. Basic pub given to long evenings of vivid conversation, dominoes and bountiful pints of golden ale. 01285 720242

Chipping Campden, Eight Bells Inn, Church St. C14 inn full of rustic charm contrasts well with modern cuisine and bright bedrooms. Fresh fare. B&B.   01386 840371
www.eightbellsinn.co.uk

Ford, Plough Inn. The first pub my 90-year old Grandmother entered, and surprisingly, she was mightily impressed at how civil and well behaved everyone was. She was there for the asparagus. Its all flagstone floors, beams and old-worlde charm. 01386 584215
www.theploughinnatford.co.uk

Great Tew, Falkland Arms. A traditional pub with flagstone floors, oak beams, inglenook fireplace, mugs and brica- brac hanging from the ceiling, and real ale in many potions to whet your senses. Garden. Accommodation with attractive bedrooms, two with 4-posters. 01608 683653
www.falklandarms.org.uk

Great Wolford, Fox & Hounds. A proper old-fashioned pub with hearty food and local ales, log fires and garden terrace. Children and pets welcome. Closed Mondays except East and Aug BHs. En-suite rooms. 01608 674220
www.thefoxandhoundsinn.com

Slad, Woolpack Inn. Traditional Cotswold pub with food simply cooked, and home to a cup of Rosie's cider and the spirit of Laurie Lee. Newspaper, views, cricketers...bliss. 01452 813429

Stow, Kings Arms, The Square. Fine pub in Market Square set on two levels. Lively and comfortable matched by well prepared ingredients. Greene King and Hook Norton beers. Children & dogs welcome. B&B.   01451 830364
www.thekingsarmsstow.co.uk

Swinbrook, Swan Inn. Owned (and visited often) by the Dowager Duchess of Devonshire (the former Deborah Mitford, the last of the infamous Mitford sisters). A beautiful pub, in a delightful location, with a good balance between traditional and modern cuisine.   01993 823339
www.theswanswinbrook.co.uk

CAFÉS / DELIS / TEAS

Broadway, Tisanes, 21 The Green. This is your traditional Cotswold tearoom set in an C17 building full of olde-fashioned charm. Garden. Walkers and dogs welcomed. Open daily 10-5. 01386 853296
www.tisanes-tearoms.co.uk

Broadway Tower, Morris & Brown. This is a new Eating Out and shopping experience. The old barn has been re-branded and converted into a posh, top-notch café-restaurant with flagstone floors, log fires and quality gifts. Open daily. 01386 852390
www.morrisandbrown.co.uk

Burford, Huffkins, High Street. This was established in 1890 and cream teas are their speciality, as are their baked produce. Such has been their success that they have recently opened in Cheltenham, Stow and Witney.

Cirencester, Made By Bob, Corn Hall. This busy food emporium opens for breakfast at 07.30, and is awash with Ciren's Ladies of Means, thereafter, in a frenzy of excitement organizing their champagne cocktails and made-up TV dinners. www.foodmadebybob.com

Filkins, Cotswold Woollen Weavers. I never tire of their homemade soups and fresh bread. Simple and fulfilling, and you may spy the eccentric owner, Richard, who will regale you with Cotswold lore and tales of yonder. Open daily. www.cotswoldwoollenweavers.co.uk

Lower Slaughter, The Old Mill. On a clear summer's day you can sit al fresco beside the Mill Pond and dream of England's pastoral glory, or enjoy their ploughman's lunch or dig into a cream tea. Open daily. www.oldmill-lowerslaughter.com

Nailsworth, William's Fish Market, Foodhall & Oyster Bar, 3 Fountain Street. In need of a sandwich for lunch, or perhaps some Sea Bass to take home to your loved home, or an oyster and a celebratory glass of bubbly. Opens at 08.00 M-Sa. 01453 832240

Tetbury, Blue Zucchini, Church Street. Just the place to spot Royal passers-by, and to enjoy a coffee break, a light lunch and meeting up with friends. 01666 505852

Winchcombe, Juris, High Street. A traditional English tearoom with a Japanese flavour set in an enchanting Grade II listed building. Open Th-Su. T 01242 602469 www.juris-tearoom.co.uk

Woodstock, Hampers Food & Wine Company, Oxford Street. I always stop here for lunch when in Woodstock; a busy deli with a wide range of sandwiches, paninis, cakes, add a relaxed ambience. T 01993 811535 www.hampersfoodandwine.co.uk

CAMP SITES

Bourton-On-The-Water, Cotswold Farm Park. A recent development with 40 pitches on a two-acre level, grassy site. All the expected mod cons are provided plus a shop stocking freshly baked bread and local farm produce. Adam's Kitchen also offers homemade cakes, light lunches and snacks. And, you have moo cows to wake you up, and the odd Cock crowing. 01451 850307 www.cotswoldfarmpark.co.uk

Charlbury, Cotswold View Caravan & Camping Park. A popular, well-run site midst the Oxfordshire Cotswolds. All within 54 acres of rolling, wooded farmland. Ideal for walking, cycling and touring the many attractions close by. Tennis court. Shop. 01608 810314 www.cotswoldview.co.uk

Cirencester, Organic Farm Shop, Burford Road. A Green Field site with Lovely views set within this organic farm. Their dictum 'Eating organic is eating from the Earth, Back to nature void of pesticides. All growing freely without insecticides.' Café. 01285 640441 www.theorganicfarmshop.co.uk

Coates, Tunnel House Inn. A rural pub with a great ambience, fine ales and yummy food has a number of small pitches and lies in an idyllic location beside the Thames and Severn Canal. Childrens play area. Dogs welcome. 01285 770280 www.tunnelhouse.com

Denfurlong Farm, Chedworth. A basic site on a green field takes you back to nature. No showers. Dogs allowed. Cheap. Café.

Eastington, Apple Tree Park. New camping and caravan site with 100 pitches in 6 acres a mile from the A38 suitable for exploring the west Cotswolds. 07708 22145

Folly Farm Campsite, Nr Bourton-On-The-Water. Set high on the Central Wolds in a drafty and healthy spot. Ideal for tents and the simple life. Don't expect 5 star accommodation. 01451 820285 www.cotswoldcamping.net

Northleach, Far Peak Camping. A simple campsite set in the middle of the Cotswolds, beside the Roman Fosse Way, and all within walking distance of Northleach. 01285 720858 www.farpeakcamping.co.uk

Nymspfield, Thistledown Environment Centre. An organic camp site that promotes the awareness of agricultural and environmental practices by tackling ecological issues head on in a fun way. Follow the adventure, sculpture and wildlife trails. Dogs allowed. 01453 860420 www.thistledown.org.uk

Winchcombe, Hayles Fruit Farm. Set in a quiet rural location beside Hailes Abbey and the Cotswold Way, so ideal for backpackers. Café/farm shop, on site. T 01242 602123 www.haylesfruitfarm.co.uk

Banbury
Spiceball Park Road   OX16 2PQ
banbury.tic@cherwell-dc.gov.uk
01295 259855

Bath
Abbey Chambers
Abbey Church Yard   BA1 1LY
tourism@bathtourism.co.uk
0906 711 2000

Bourton-on-the-Water
Victoria Street   GL54 2BU
bourtonvic@btconnect.com
01451 820 211

Bradford-on-Avon
The Greenhouse
50 St. Margaret's Street   BA15 1DE
tic@bradfordonavon.co.uk
01225 865797

Broadway
Unit 14 Russell Square
High Street   WR12 7AP
01386 852 937

Burford
33A High Street   OX18 4QA
burford.vic@westoxon.gov.uk
01993 823 558

Cheltenham Municipal Offices
77 Promenade   GL50 1PJ
info@cheltenham.gov.uk
01242 522 878

Chippenham
Yelde Hall
Market Place   SN15 3HL
tourism@chippenham.gov.uk
01249 665 970

Chipping Campden
The Old Police Station
High Street   GL55 6HB
visitchippingcampden@lineone.net
01386 841 206

Cirencester
Corinium Museum
Park Street   GL7 2BX
cirencestervic@cotswold.gov.uk
01285 655 611

Corsham
Arnold House
31 High Street   SN13 0EZ
enquiries@corshamheritage.org.uk
01249 714 660

Evesham
The Almonry
Abbey Gate   WR11 4BG
tic@almonry.ndo.co.uk
01386 446 944

Gloucester
28 Southgate Street   GL1 2DP
tourism@gloucester.gov.uk
01452 396 572

Moreton-in-Marsh
Moreton Area Centre
High Street   GL56 0AZ
moreton@cotswold.gov.uk
01608 650 881

Nailsworth
The Old George
George Street   GL6 0AQ
01453 839222

Painswick
The Library
Stroud Road   GL6 6UT
01452 813552

Pershore
Town Hall
34 High Street   WR10 1DS
tourism@pershore-tc.gov.uk
01386 556 591

Stow-On-The-Wold
Cotswold Cricket Museum
Brewery Yard
Sheep Street   GL54 1AA
www.cotswoldcricketmuseum.co.uk
01451 870083

Stroud
Subscription Rooms
George Street   GL5 1AE
tic@stroud.gov.uk
01453 760 960

Tetbury
33 Church Street   GL8 8JG
tourism@tetbury.org
01666 503 552
Seasonal opening

Tewkesbury
Out of the Hat Tewkesbury
Heritage & Visitor Centre
100 Church Street   GL20 5AB
tewkesburytic@tewkesbury.gov.uk
01684 855 040

Upton Upon Severn
4 High Street   WR8 0HB
upton.tic@malvernhills.gov.uk
01684 594200

Winchcombe
Town Hall
High Street   GL54 5LJ
winchcombetic@tewkesbury.gov.uk
01242 602 925
Seasonal opening

Witney
26a Market Square   OX28 6BB
witney.vic@westoxon.gov.uk
01993 775802

Wotton-under-Edge
The Heritage Centre
The Chipping   GL12 7AD
01453 521541

CALENDAR OF EVENTS

January
Gloucester Cajun & Zydeco Festival
Royal Shakespeare season ends

February
Snowdrops at Colesbourne Park
Snowdrops at Rococo Gardens, Painswick

March
Cheltenham National Hunt Festival
Chipping Norton Music Festival
Evesham Spring Regatta
Lambing, Cotswold Farm Park
Royal Shakespeare Theatre season begins
West Country Game Fair, Royal Bath & West
Showground

April
Adderbury Day of (Morris) Dance www.adderbury.
org
Broadway Spring point-to-point
Cheltenham International Jazz Festival
Cirencester Beer Festival
Evesham Vintage Easter Gathering
Great Blenheim Palace Easter Egg Challenge
GWR Toddington Spring Diesel Gala
Nailsworth Festival
Highnam Court Spring Fair
Shakespeare Birthday celebrations, Stratford
Stratford-Upon-Avon Literary Festival

May
Badminton Horse Trials
Banbury Beer Festival
Bath International Music Festival
Burford Levellers Day
Chipping Campden Music Festival
Clipping the yews, Painswick
Coopers Hill Cheese Rolling
Dover's Olympick Games, Chipping Campden
Gloucester Tall Ships Festival
Kemble Great Vintage Flying Weekend
Malvern Arts Festival
Malvern Spring Gardening Show
Pershore Carnival
Prescott Hill Classic Car Event
Randwick Cheese Rolling
South Cerney Street Fair BH M
Stow Horse Fair
Tetbury Woolsack Races BH M
Tewkesbury Festival of Food & Drink (&Merriment)
Tortworth Vintage Rally
Upton Folk Festival
Wychwood Music Festival, Cheltenham Racecourse

June
Banbury Show
Bledington Music Festival
Bloxham Steam Rally
Cheltenham Science Festival
Deddington Festival
Gloucester Medieval Fayre
Kemble Air Day
Longborough Festival Opera
Pershore Festival of Arts
Severn Project
Sudeley Castle Rose Week
Three Counties Agricultural Show, Malvern

July
Banbury Hobby Horse Festival
Cornbury Music Festival, Charlbury
Cotswold Show, Cirencester Park
Fairford Air Tattoo
Fairport Convention, Cropredy
Gloucester Festival
Gloucester Rhythm & Blues Festival
Hook Norton Fetsival of Fine Ales
Music Deo Sacra, Tewkesbury Abbey
Music At The Crossroads, Hook Norton

August
Bourton Water Games BH M
Evesham Flower Show
Prescott Vintage Hill Climb
Three Choirs Festival
Winchcombe Flower Show
September
Banbury Cavalcade of Sport
Battle of Britain Weekend, Kemble Airfield
Cheltenham Carnival
Chipping Norton Mop Fair
Moreton-in-Marsh Show

October
Banbury Canal Day
Cheltenham Literary Festival
Shipston Medieval Fun Fair
Stratford Mop Fair
Tewkesbury Mop Fair
Westonbirt Arboretum's Autumn Colours

November
Bonfire Show, Cheltenham Racecourse

December
Christmas Carol Service, Gloucester Cathedral